THE SAGA FO

# The
# Saga Food Guide

**Carol J. Leverkus,** BSc, SRD

UNWIN
PAPERBACKS

LONDON SYDNEY WELLINGTON

First published in Great Britain by Unwin Paperbacks,
an imprint of Unwin Hyman Limited, 1988.
© Carol Leverkus 1988

**Unwin Hyman Limited**
15–17 Broadwick Street, London W1V 1FP

Allen & Unwin Australia Pty Ltd
8 Napier Street, North Sydney, NSW 2060, Australia

Allen & Unwin New Zealand Pty Ltd with the Port Nicholson Press
60 Cambridge Terrace, Wellington, New Zealand

**British Library Cataloguing in Publication Data**

Leverkus, Carol
  Saga food guide.
  1. Food. For old persons
  I. Title II. Series
  641.3
  ISBN 0–04–440173–6

Set in 11 on 12½ point Plantin by Computape (Pickering) Ltd.
and printed in Great Britain by
Cox & Wyman Ltd, Reading

# CONTENTS

# INTRODUCTION

Retirement may represent the first period since child-hood of freedom to express one's own personality and to tackle life at one's own pace. The persistent demands of a full-time job and bringing up a family tend to leave little opportunity to explore new foods and recipes or to examine one's lifestyle in relation to health.

Health is a vital ingredient for enjoying all the opportunities that retirement can offer. For this reason, this book provides basic information and advice on nutrition and diet in relation to health. It will help you make wise food choices that lead to a long and healthy retirement.

One of the most common concerns in later life is that of keeping slim. This is not surprising when about half the population around retirement age is overweight. Apart from the important consideration of appearance, it can aggravate many health problems. But with more time to cook and plan meals from healthy basic ingre-dients, and to take exercise, overweight can be easily tackled.

Surely one of the most appealing aspects of retirement is the availability of time which allows us to approach life in a calmer fashion. Time provides many opportunities, such as shopping for good value and quality, growing fresh herbs or vegetables and gather-ing wild produce like blackberries or bilberries. Time to experiment with new foods and combinations of ingredients in a relaxed way can also provide enormous fun. After all, if you are cooking for one or two without a strict timetable, it is not too serious if things don't turn out quite as expected!

The greater freedom of retirement will probably open up opportunities for outings and entertaining, so these two topics are considered in the book, as well as cooking for the endearing grandchildren. With more time to plan healthy meals, while relying on fewer convenience foods, retired grandparents are in an excellent position to set a good example – as well as reaping the health benefits themselves.

As finance is often a major concern in retirement, cost has been considered throughout the book. For those particularly concerned about their budgets, specific ideas are provided on shopping and cooking economically.

For couples it makes much more sense for the activity of cooking to be shared. There are two reasons. First, women, like men, need to enjoy their retirement and not find that their work is actually increased as a result of cooking more meals. Second, men never know when their cooking skills may suddenly be called upon, due to the death or illness of their wife. It is much easier to learn new skills when approaching, or in, early retirement. Trying to cope with cooking (when lacking experience) on top of a domestic crisis is a sure way to a poor diet and resulting ill health. For many people who have previously had little chance to spend time in the kitchen, it can be extremely exhilarating to discover new and creative skills in cooking.

After years of hard work and rushed meals, what could be more enjoyable than to relax over an attractive and tasty meal – in the knowledge that it's doing you good!

**Note**: In the recipes, measures are level unless otherwise stated.

# 1 BASIC NUTRITION KNOW-HOW

## Is Nutritional Advice Always Changing?

Basic knowledge of nutrition really starts in the food shops, vegetable garden and the kitchen and not from a good grasp of which vitamins, minerals and trace elements do what. The most nutritious diets can emanate from common sense built on a sound foundation from childhood.

Contrary to popular belief, the basics of choosing and preparing a healthy diet have changed very little over the years. The knowledge that it is best to choose a wide variety of food and avoid excesses and waste has been with us for generations. Sound nutrition guidelines advocated during the Second World War still hold true today. The emphasis on nutritional advice has, however, altered with changes in our society.

## New Priorities

Think back to the 1930s and during the war when nutritional deficiency was a major concern. 'Eat up all your meat' was a valuable phrase for the thirties when poverty meant that protein was in short supply for many families. Increased wealth and the improved availability of food, through efficient transport and storage, has meant there is now an abundance of protein foods and vitamin-rich vegetables and fruits throughout the year. On the other hand, the growth of low-price processed foods, take-away meals and ready-to-eat foods has led to dietary excesses. Hence advice today concentrates on the problems of excess fat, sugar and salt and insufficient fibre. By adjusting these dietary factors the quality of the diet also improves in terms of vital vitamins and minerals.

## Nutrition in Later Life

Throughout life, wise choice of foods is a key to good health. However, just as our food supply and eating habits have changed over our lifetimes, so too, with age, come subtle changes in our nutritional requirements.

The most important consideration is that of avoiding the loss of lean body tissue, usually with a resulting rise in the percentage of fat in the body. The body becomes less muscular and the metabolic rate (a measure of the amount of energy or calories you need from food) declines. A word of warning is needed here, however: reduced physical activity (a key feature of the middle and later years) may be the main factor leading to the loss of body muscle and the tendency to gain weight. And, of course, it must be remembered that exercise itself burns up extra calories.

Although on growing older less energy – that is, fewer calories – is required from food (unless physical activity and lean body tissue are maintained, an older person requires the basic nutrients in similar amounts to a young adult. When large quantities of food are needed, the sheer volume consumed usually safeguards against nutritional deficiency. However, with a falling appetite and energy requirement, the quality of food becomes the vital issue. Extra care when choosing food may also be needed to balance a less efficient use of certain nutrients such as iron, calcium and some vitamins. So some basic knowledge of nutrition can stand you in good stead.

Changes imposed by requirement provide an excellent opportunity for questioning your lifestyle. Those approaching, or in, early retirement are among the most interested and searching on the subject of food and health. One study, carried out in 1981 on people approaching retirement, showed that all the participants had changed their diet over the previous year.

Making meals a bit simpler if you are just catering for one or two is fine, but you need to have the basic principles in mind. Whether a meal comprises an elaborate hot dish or a simple cold platter makes little difference nutritionally. What matters is that your meals provide a wide range of vitamins and minerals along with protein, essential fats and carbohydrates, fibre and water.


## General Principles

For simplicity's sake, foods which supply similar nutrients are conventionally grouped together. For most people a food from each group listed below needs to be eaten, in some form, about three times a day. This will supply, over a period of time, all the nutrients the body requires. The three main groups are:

1  *Vegetables and fruits* – vital for vitamins C and folate (a B vitamin), fibre and essential minerals.
2  *Carbohydrate or starchy foods*, e.g. potatoes, cereals, bread – vital for many B vitamins, minerals (e.g. iron) and fibre.
3  *Protein foods*  (a)  Meat, fish, eggs, nuts, beans,

peas, lentils – rich in protein, many B vitamins, iron and other minerals. (b) Milk, yogurt, cheese – major sources of calcium, protein and some vitamins.

As well as providing the building material for the body's tissues, the protein foods are responsible for the maintenance of healthy bones and blood. Half a pint (300 ml) of milk a day in drinks and in cooking, plus a little cheese and yogurt some days, is a good target for which to aim. For those who do not like milk, a small carton of yogurt or 1 oz (25 g) of cheese is equivalent to about ⅓ pint (180 ml) of milk.

*Water*
Water is a vital part of the diet. About 2 pints (1 litre) of water or other fluids are required per day to keep the body healthy. Hard water may help to protect against heart disease, so avoid having your drinking water softened.

*Regular Meals?*
Regular meals are a good idea as a means of getting into a sensible dietary pattern. Fasting and then feasting usually result in weight problems and an increased risk of over- and under-indulgence in certain nutrients. Moreover, upsets resulting from ill health or a bereavement can be coped with better if there is a regular pattern to follow – especially when an interest in food may be temporarily lost.

Without the restrictions of a working day, it is easier in retirement to have the main meal at mid-day, which can then be worked off during the rest of the day. Something lighter can be taken in the evening. But it is really a matter of personal choice how you arrange your meals.

There is nothing wrong with the following regular

meal plan if it suits your lifestyle (even though it may seem upside-down to many people!): a brunch of something on toast and fruit late morning, followed by a main meal around 5 pm and a bowl of cereal and milk at bedtime.

## Nutrients for Special Attention
Try to plan your meals making good use of the foods listed below. They are valuable for those nutrients that you need to be particularly careful of including in your diet to maintain good health.

NUTRIENT

GOOD SOURCES

### Calcium
Fractures and osteoporosis (lack of bone density and calcium) are common in later life, particularly in women. Osteoporosis is thought to occur in one in four women over sixty-five years of age in the United Kingdom. Maintaining a good intake of calcium throughout life (especially, if you are a woman, after the menopause) makes sound sense. (See also vitamin D).

Milk, cheese, yogurt.
Canned fish (with bones).
Bread, flour.
Hard water.

### Iron
Iron is required for the red pigment in blood which transports oxygen around the body. Lack of iron can result in anaemia and feeling exhausted from an oxygen shortage. (See also vitamin C and folate).

Red meat, especially liver, kidneys.
Pulses, green vegetables.
Bread, cereals especially wholegrain.
Cocoa, dried fruit.
Eggs.

### Essential fats
Some fats known as essential fatty acids (EFAs) are vital for the growth and maintenance of tissues and for healthy skin. However, although a deficiency of EFAs can contribute to poor skin, taking large quantities is unlikely to cure skin problems. Another fatty acid found in fish oils may help to protect against thrombosis.

Oily fish, e.g. mackerel, tuna, herrings, etc.
Vegetable oils.
Nuts and seeds.

# THE SAGA FOOD GUIDE

## Vitamin A

Helps to maintain healthy eyes, night sight and skin. Betacarotene, which is converted to vitamin A in the body, comes from many fruits and vegetables and may help to prevent cancer. Carcinogens must be oxidised before they can damage body cells. Betacarotene can help to prevent this oxidation.

Margarine, milk, cheese.
Liver, egg yolk.
Green vegetables.
Yellow and red vegetables and fruits, such as carrots and apricots.
Fish oils.

## Folic acid (folate – a B vitamin)*

Folic acid, like iron, helps to maintain healthy blood, preventing anaemia. It is also essential for building the body's tissues and preventing tiredness and depression. Like vitamin C it is easily destroyed during cooking and storage and is not kept in the body for long.

Green vegetables, parsnips.
Egg yolk.
Liver, kidneys.
Yeast and meat extract.
Pulses (i.e. peas, beans, lentils).
Fruit – especially oranges, bananas, melons.

## Vitamin C*

Vitamin C helps the iron in food to be absorbed – so a salad with a chop, or a glass of orange juice with a boiled egg, is a good combination. It also helps to fight infection generally. When cooking for just one or two it is all too easy to neglect vegetables, which require regular shopping, but it is well worth the effort to prepare and cook them even for small numbers.

Citrus fruit – oranges, grapefruit, satsumas and their juices.
Other fruit – fresh pineapple, bananas and berry fruit.
Vegetables – cabbage, sprouts, greens, cauliflower, new potatoes, tomatoes.

## Vitamin D

Vitamin D helps calcium to be absorbed from food. In Britain the major source is from the action of sunlight on the skin. If you don't go out in the sunlight much or tend not to expose your skin to the sun, the food sources become important. People who take a holiday in the sun each year or eat oily fish at least once a week are unlikely to go short of the vitamin.

Oily fish, eggs.
The following have vitamin D added – check the labelling for details: margarine, some natural yogurts, evaporated milk, Ovaltine, some breakfast cereals.

* You should be particularly watchful that your diet includes both vitamin C and folic acid in sufficient quantities.

## Clever Shopping

The key to getting the maximum enjoyment from food starts at the shops. The art of economically shopping to obtain a healthy selection of exciting food with the minimum of effort is a skill that develops with experience. Nonetheless, even for the most experienced shopper, there is a wealth of new foods and types of packaging to keep abreast of and so many factors to balance: 'Is the food tasty?'; 'Is it healthy or suitable for my special diet?'; 'Is it easy to cook?'; 'Is it good value?'; 'How long will it keep?'; and so on. Particularly for those new to shopping it is worth checking how your practices measure up to the following guidelines.

### *When and Where to Shop*
When and where to shop is governed by your local facilities and transport arrangements, so only general guidelines can be provided.

- Shopping at a large supermarket for most commodities should give the best value (even allowing for the cost of transport), as well as a guarantee of freshness. Good parking facilities that avoid the need to carry heavy shopping are obviously a key factor too. Unless such a shop is very convenient, visiting it once a week or fortnight should be sufficient.
- Small local shops, involving no travel, can be useful for supplying small quantities, allowing you to select the exact one or two chops, chicken pieces or fish fillets that you want. If a standard supermarket pack supplies more than you need, there is no saving even if it is cheaper per pound. Other foods with a short shelf life, like cottage cheese, yogurt

9

and bread can conveniently be bought from small local shops between the major shopping trips.

- Vegetables and fruit are normally best value from a reliable market stall, farm shop or greengrocer with a fast turn-over of stock. However, shopping for just one or two items – say, a couple of high-quality onions – at a large supermarket may result in less waste and subsequent savings.

- Your life may be so busy with clubs, hobbies and commitments that you have to fit in shopping when you can, but try to benefit from two opportunities. Shops have slack periods at the start of the week, often mid-morning or early afternoon, when shopping can be done restfully in a fraction of the time. (Early in the morning or late in the day the shelves are often poorly stocked.) Sell-by dates on particular perishable items generally expire on the same day each week. You can pick up good bargains by timing your shopping expeditions accordingly. Only buy an item reduced for quick sale because its sell-by date has been reached if you can eat it all within a day, of course. You can freeze such items, provided that you use them within a day once defrosted.

- Provided you have access to a large supermarket there should be little need to use expensive specialist shops such as delicatessens. The large chains are now stocking more exotic foods where the demand is sufficient. Don't be shy of asking the supermarket manager or appropriate section manager if there is something you would like them to stock.

- Shopping at a health food shop is not a passport to a healthy diet. There is an abundance of competitively priced, healthy, basic foods available at large supermarkets today. Sometimes, however, muesli (without added sugar) and wholegrain cereal flakes (for instance, maize, rye, oats or wheat) are cheaper or only available at health food shops. Check the price, type and quality of fruit juices, nuts, pulses, herbal teas and wholegrain flours, pastas and rice at the supermarket before buying them at the health food shop.

- When shopping at a market there can be great bargains at the end of the day, but these must be balanced against the better-quality produce being available early. In hot or frosty weather fruit and vegetables, sold outdoors, can of course deteriorate during the day.

*Getting Value for Money*
- Always write a shopping list based on a rough idea of what you plan to cook until the next major shopping trip. This prevents expensive impulse buys. Allow some flexibility when shopping – for example, peppers might be particularly expensive one week and perhaps they could be replaced by leeks. Un-expected good buys arise, but if you are on a limited budget, buy these unplanned items in place of another food or to build up your store cupboard.

- When buying foods on special offer, check their sell-by dates, quality and pack size to make sure that they are the bargain they claim to be.
- The cheapest foods are not always the best value. Lean mince and low-fat sausages may cost more per pound but they go further as there is less fat to discard. Some low-priced chickens provide little meat when served as they contain a high proportion of fat and water, which is lost in cooking.
- Don't be had by foods sold in fancy packaging or marketed for 'health' or for festive occasions. These can have a high price mark-up and be bad value. Something very similar may be sold in a different format far more cheaply.
- Large packets can sometimes have very small contents! Check the weight for the price on packets as the packaging can be so misleading. Sometimes even smaller or medium-size packets on special offer can be cheaper per pound than large ones.
- Supermarkets' 'own label' products are usually a good choice, representing value for money – unless, in some instances, you find the quality inferior to that of branded products.
- Apart from checking the weight on a food, look at the ingredients list to see what you are paying for. Terms like 'beef flavour' or 'tomato flavour' can be most misleading. They do not mean you will find beef or tomato in the products. Expensive health foods and products can claim to be 'no added sugar' or 'free from animal fat', but on reading the label you may detect honey and a hydrogenated vegetable oil. Honey is, after all, just sugar plus about a quarter water. Hydrogenated oils can be hard saturated fats with no benefits to health compared with animal fats.
- When buying products from the market, par-

ticularly fruit and vegetables, check their quality before putting them in your shopping bag. Have no qualms about asking for a replacement if an item is clearly inferior.

## What about Food Labelling?

It can be difficult to eat healthily and get value for money if you do not know what foods contain. Fortunately changes are afoot to improve food labelling so we will know more about the nutritional content of food. Sadly these changes have been slow, due to the difficulty in obtaining agreement between the Ministry of Agriculture, Fisheries and Food, the food industry and those representing the consumers' interest.

### Names

As things stand, prepacked foods and most non-prepacked foods must show the name of the food on the label. Some names are 'prescribed' by law – such as wholemeal bread or pilchards. Other foods have what are termed 'customary' names, such as fish fingers or Chelsea buns. Foods that have neither of these types of names have a 'descriptive' one, for example 'red kidney beans in chilli sauce'. These descriptive names need to be precise enough to distinguish them from similar products. Frequently a trade mark or brand name precedes the descriptive name. The labelling should also make it clear to the consumer the form in which the food is sold: for example, whether it is dried, reconstituted, stored in brine and so on.

The laws on food labelling help to protect us against misleading names. For example, if a yogurt carton has a picture of blackcurrants on it or is named 'blackcurrant' or 'blackcurrant-flavoured', then the flavour must come mainly from blackcurrants. On the other hand the words 'blackcurrant flavour' mean the flavour comes mainly from artificial flavourings so do not be surprised when you find no fruit inside the carton. It is worth looking out for terms like 'beef flavour' or 'chicken flavour', particularly if you are expecting a product labelled as such to provide a substantial meal. You will not find the meat you may be desiring for your main meal.

## The Ingredients List

Probably the most useful part of the label at the present time is the ingredients list. Most prepacked foods must have this list. The ingredients on labels are shown in descending order of weight, which gives a good indication of what you are paying for. Most additives are indicated on the ingredients list. For more information on additives see page 48. In a beef curry or bolognaise sauce one can quickly assess whether the beef is a major or a subsidiary ingredient. It can be a revelation to find out that water, flour or edible starch is the main ingredient. When comparing brands it can be extremely useful to discover, through the ingredients list, that one product has sugar as the first ingredient or salt very high up the list whereas another has fruit listed first or salt as virtually the last ingredient.

The ingredients list can be invaluable to vegetarians and people on special diets such as diabetics, or those with a known food intolerance or food allergy.

Another aspect of the ingredients list is that water only needs to be declared when it makes up more than 5% of the finished weight.

One weakness of the ingredients list is where an ingredient, used in the labelled product, has been previously processed or treated. One example could be dried fruit, that has been coated in a mineral oil and then used in a fruit loaf. This mineral oil would not be declared in the final product. It is easy for additives to be missed off an ingredients list in this way.

A precaution to take when interpreting an ingredients list is to check whether several similar ingredients are listed. For example, when comparing two types of vegetable soup, brand A may have used 12 types of vegetables and brand B only 3. As a result the product with the 12 vegetables may have flour or starch listed first whereas the other soup may have a vegetable listed first. This can be the case even though the total amount of vegetable may be lower in brand B than in brand A. Another misleading example is where sugar is listed several times, but expressed in different ways, such as 'sugar', then 'glucose syrup' followed by 'maltose'. All of these types of sugar can appear fairly low down the ingredients list, but added together could make sugar the major ingredient.

*Nutritional Labelling*
Because of the short-comings of the ingredients list, nutritional labelling is obviously useful, telling us how much fat, protein, sugar, salt and certain vitamins and minerals a product supplies. But here too some care is required with interpretation. It can be easy to argue that oven chips do not provide much fat compared to a low fat spread. The only trouble is we do not expect the vegetables in our diet to contribute much fat whereas we do expect meat, cheese and animal and vegetable fats and oils to be major contributors. Another important issue is the weight of a portion. A helping of the chips is likely to be 12 times the weight of a portion of margarine. We therefore need to compare like with like – one spreading fat with another and sausages with chicken, chops or fish fingers. The quantity of the product you are likely to consume also needs to be

considered. For example fresh parsley may be advocated as an excellent source of vitamin C, but sadly, in the quantities in which it is usually eaten, the contribution is virtually negligible.

One area of confusion can be that of expressing nutritional content in terms of dry or wet weight. In the case of many cheeses you will find some fat contents expressed as a percentage of dry weight and others expressed as a percentage of the weight as eaten or the wet weight. Where the fat content is expressed as a percentage of the dry weight it will appear much higher than when quoted in terms of the wet weight.

## Date Marks

Most foods carry a date mark if the minimum shelf life is less than 18 months. There are exceptions, including fresh fruit and vegetables which have not been peeled or cut into pieces. Other exceptions include ices and confectionery normally eaten within 12 hours of being made.

The date marking differs depending on the minimum shelf life. Food with a shelf life greater than three months must have a mark indicating the end of the month and year by which the food must be eaten. For foods with less than a three month shelf life the day and month by which the food should be eaten is required. Where 'sell-by' dates are used instead of a date mark, these must also state within how many days of purchase the food should be eaten.

With the advent of the new food labelling regulations it can only be hoped that good educational material will be made widely available to the general public, so that the information can be accurately interpreted.

## The Basic Store Cupboard

*Foods with Good Shelf Life*
Wholegrain breakfast cereals, oats
Fine wholemeal self-raising flour
White and wholemeal plain flours (if you make bread or
    pastries)
Wholegrain crispbreads
Wholegrain pasta (e) and rice
Tinned fish (e)
Dried lentils or beans
Tinned beans, e.g. baked beans (e) or kidney beans
Unsalted nuts (e)
Dried or long-life milk (e)
Tinned tomatoes, tomato purée
Long-life fruit juice
Tinned fruit in natural juice (e)
Sugar (raw cane sugar for extra flavour and nutrients),
    artificial sweetener
Corn, rape-seed, soya or sunflower oil
Margarine high in polyunsaturates or reduced-fat
    spread
Wine or cider vinegar
Stock cubes, mixed herbs, curry powder
Garlic
Mixed spice, ginger, nutmeg, cinnamon, vanilla
    flavouring
Coffee, tea or other favourite beverage

*Fresh Foods*
Semi-skimmed milk
Reduced-fat or medium-fat hard cheese, low-fat soft
    cheese, natural yogurt
Eggs (e)
Wholemeal bread
Potatoes, onions

One or two other fresh vegetables and fruits with
  moderate shelf life.
A vegetable and a fruit for quick eating
Salad vegetables
Fresh fish, lean red meat, offal or poultry
Frozen fish, meat, vegetables and fruit (if a freezer is
  available)
Frozen nut or soya bean burgers – suitable for vege-
  tarians

The foods marked with (e) are particularly recommended for emergencies when time or energy are
lacking or the fresh variety has run out. Other suggestions for foods that are quick to prepare are listed on
page 68, and a list of useful pre-prepared foods to stock
is provided on page 69.

Some foods, such as tinned fish, represent particularly
good value for money. These good-value foods are
itemized on page 76. Some of the newer foods that are
helpful in improving the healthiness of the British diet
are recommended in chapters 4, 5 and 6.

*Shopping for New and More Adventurous Foods*
Practising the shopping tips on getting value for money
as well as acquainting yourself with the good-value
specialities in your locality should allow scope for
trying some more adventurous foods – even if you are
on a tight budget. It is always best to try the more exotic
seasonal foods in their main season, so they are at their
lowest price, for example aubergines, courgettes,
fennel, avocados, kiwi fruit, sharon fruit. More adventurous foods to stock, for adding a little extra flair to
your meals, are suggested on page 111.
  When encountering new chilled foods such as low-fat
soft cheeses or prepared fish, chicken or pasta dishes, it

is wise to check their sell-by dates. Before making any unplanned purchases make sure that you can use them in time unless they are suitable for freezing.

*Hints for Shopping for One or Two*
- Check whether it is cheaper to use small shops, such as a butcher or greengrocer, which charge the same price per pound regardless of the quantity purchased. This is particularly relevant to fresh fruit, vegetables, meat and fish. Supermarkets often charge more per pound for small packs or will not sell small packs at all.
- Try to buy medium to large packs and plan different meals based on the same ingredients. The following are examples of versatile foods that can be used in different ways: lean mince, whole chicken, bacon hock joint, white cabbage, natural yogurt, fromage frais, celery, cauliflower. See 'Variety from the Same Ingredients' on page 33.
- Some economy packs of foods such as margarine, rice, muesli, nuts, apples or potatoes can easily be shared with neighbours.
- When buying perishable foods to cover several meals, always look for the packet with the latest sell-by date. If the food you have in mind is to be eaten within just a day or two, it is probably better to buy something else.
- The following fruit and vegetables store reasonably well when kept cool, so don't need a large family to eat them quickly: apples, beetroot, carrots, celery, chicory, Chinese leaf, citrus fruit, courgettes, Dutch cabbage, garlic, Iceberg, Cos and Webbs lettuce, leeks, marrow, mustard and cress, onions, parsnips, potatoes, swedes, turnips.
- Some fruit and vegetables, like bananas, berry fruits, pears, plums, peppers and tomatoes (unless

they are of exceptional quality), can deteriorate quickly, so consider buying in just ¼ or ½ lb (125–250 g) quantities. Cucumbers can quickly lose freshness, so buying in halves can work out cheaper. Round lettuces and watercress may be best avoided unless you can use them within one or two days.

- A freezer is invaluable when shopping and cooking for small numbers (see page 34).
- Buying fresh herbs can work out expensive when only small quantities are required, so try growing your own, outdoors or indoors.
- For those who like a little drink with some meals, wine can work out expensive when a whole bottle needs to be opened. Alternatives include wine boxes, cider, small cans of beer or montilla with a dash of sparkling mineral water. Cider, montilla and sparkling mineral water do deteriorate on opening, but can be kept for at least a week. Remember to replace their caps immediately after opening. If you feel that a wine box will tempt you to drink more than you would otherwise, it is probably not the best suggestion! A Vacu-vin – a wine-sealing gadget available from some department stores and off licences – may be worth considering. This allows you to recork a wine bottle after drinking just a glass or two. It removes the air from the bottle so that the wine can be kept for a couple of weeks without deterioration.

# 2  NEW TO COOKING

As cooking is an everyday activity, it is important that you enjoy it as much as possible. It may be tempting to dismiss cooking as unimportant, especially if you are catering for one. Maintaining some interest in cooking does, however, help to safeguard against a poor diet and resulting ill health.

- Choose dishes that are easy to cook but use flavoursome ingredients. That way there is little to go wrong and you will end up with an interesting taste even if it is not quite what you intended.
- Begin preparation well before the meal time. Starting to cook when you feel the hunger pangs is a recipe for disaster. Cooking needs a relaxed, patient approach.
- It's worth spending some leisure time perusing recipes such as those in newspapers, magazines or on the back of food packets. This builds up your knowledge of what foods go with what, as well as stimulating interest in cooking.
- Recipes are there as guidelines – feel free to adapt them to what is available in your area, what is in season and to your taste and pocket. Try to substitute like for like, for instance apple for pear, or chicken for pork, or mixed spice for cinnamon.

  Think about the consequence of the change. Does the different meat need a longer or shorter time to cook? Will a different fruit or vegetable

produce more or less water, needing an adjustment to the fluid in the recipe?

- Build up your confidence in cooking. But why not cut a few corners, such as using ready-prepared tinned fruit in natural juice, tinned kidney beans or cooked ham in place of bacon? Cooking does get quicker once it becomes routine. Other ideas are included in chapter 7 (see page 67).

- Concentrate your efforts on the main course of the main meal as enjoyable desserts and snack meals can usually be produced with little or no cooking. (For example, quick snack meals can be made using interesting breads, salad items, cheeses and cold meats.)

- When choosing ingredients, think about their colour. Make meals exciting by incorporating bright green, red, yellow and orange foods.

- When halving or quartering recipes, it might be helpful to write down the altered quantity on a slip of paper. Place this over the original quantities in the recipe. Alternatively, write the adjusted figures in pencil on the recipe. When doing the maths as you go along, it's easy to make a mistake with an important ingredient such as the fat or liquid, giving a disastrous result.

- Further education classes on cooking are worth looking out for. You can learn useful skills as well as having great fun.
- Discuss cooking with friends. There is no need to feel inadequate! Everyone has a good idea to share with others, including new cooks.

## Equipment

New equipment can be daunting. But finding techniques and gadgets that suit you can make all the difference to stress-free catering.

### Basic Appliances and Utensils

If you are reviewing the equipment to have in your kitchen, the following list should provide a valuable checklist:

Grill, toaster, easily regulated hob or stove, oven (preferably with fan and at eye level)

Easy-clean heavy-bottomed or non-stick sauce pans

Casserole dishes or pans for the hob and oven (for one or two portions and for entertaining)

Non-stick deep frying pan with lid and steam vent

Baking sheet, enamel plate

Pudding basin, larger mixing bowls, bowls for salads and desserts

Sharp knives (requiring just one clean cut – far safer than blunt ones) and sharp stainless steel scissors

Spatula and cooking spoons for non-stick pans

Spatula for scraping bowls, cake/quiche slice

Grater (large metal or plastic one if you are wary of scraping your knuckles)

Sieve, colander

Timer, e.g. digital electronic one.

Large chopping board, measuring jug, measuring spoons

Hand whisk – an electric one can be useful

Plastic containers with lids, plastic bags of assorted sizes, Cling-film

Once you have found your feet in the kitchen, clear out any old equipment that you don't plan to use. Cooking is much quicker when your utensils are easy to find in uncluttered drawers and cupboards.

*Specialized Equipment*

The following more specialized pieces of equipment may well be the answer to your needs – try to look out for them in other people's homes and discuss their applications:

Microwave cooker

Infra-red grill

Slow cooker

Wok

Small food processor

Liquidizer

Steamer – with partitions for different vegetables

Pressure cooker

Hot plate – alleviates time difficulties, e.g. rice or potatoes can be kept warm while the main dish finishes cooking or *vice versa*

Non-stick cake and loaf tins, roasting tin

Grapefruit knife, garlic press.

Try to collect one or two plates and bowls with interesting shapes and pleasing colours. Even the simplest meals can look appealing when served on attractive crockery.

## Storing Food

*Cool, Dry Storage*
Most foods, if not stored in a fridge or freezer, prefer dry, cool storage. In particular, give attention to foods with a fairly high moisture content such as fresh fruit, vegetables and bread. A warm, moist atmosphere quickly leads to decay.

*Refrigeration*
The following should be kept in the fridge: meat and fish, including tinned once opened; cheese and eggs, unless you have a cool larder; milk, yogurt and cream, including long-life once opened; salad vegetables (at the bottom of the fridge); berry fruits; long-life fruit juice, once opened; foods bought chilled; jams, sauces and pickles with instructions on the container to 'refrigerate once opened', for instance pickled onions, gherkins and mayonnaise.

Remember always to keep items wrapped or covered as a fridge dries out food. However, vegetables and fruit also need to breathe, so make sure that salad items are kept in perforated plastic or paper bags.

Bananas do not like to be stored in the fridge.

## First Dishes

The following dishes are ideal for beginners.

*Savoury*
- Grilled foods, such as fish or chops cooked with herbs, lemon or lime juice, garlic and so on; cheese or fish on toast.
- Casseroles.
- Stuffed baked potatoes.

- Open sandwiches or stuffed pitta bread.
- Ploughman's snack, for instance warmed brown bread rolls with cheese, pickle and salad garnish.
- Flavoursome and colourful vegetables, such as leeks, aubergines, peppers, fennel, chicory or water cress – cooked or raw as an accompaniment or in casseroles.

*Puddings*
- Fruit salad – using a small tin of fruit in a natural juice and an interesting fresh fruit, for example a kiwi, sharon or a few grapes.
- Mixed dried fruit compote – dried fruit soaked in water with optional nuts added.
- Fruit crumble – see recipe on page 27.
- Baked apple stuffed with dried fruit, spice and a little brown sugar or honey.
- Fresh fruit or a real fruit yogurt with no added sugar.

## Clearing Up

When cooking try to use the minimum of pots, bowls and spoons and clear up as you go along. You can then relax over the meal, knowing that there is little to tackle afterwards.

After the meal, first of all deal with the left-over food. Cooked dishes should never be left out of the fridge all day or overnight as they become unsafe to eat. Cool left-over, hot food quickly. When it is nearly cold, put it covered in the fridge, either still in its cooking pot or transferred to a clean, smaller dish. When the washing up is done before this, it is quite easy to forget about the left-over food.

Provided that the dishes are tidily stacked up, there

is no need to wash up after every snack or meal. But try to wash up greasy dishes and ones which have contained meat and fish as soon after the meal as possible. The hot water can be timed accordingly. Soaking 'stubborn' pans in water is more successful after they have cooled, not as soon as they have come out of the oven or off the stove.

## Simple Recipes

### Tandoori Chicken

SERVES 2–4
2 tablespoons natural yogurt
1 tablespoon tandoori spice
   Grated rind of ½ lemon
2 teaspoons lemon juice
   Pinch of salt
4 chicken drumsticks

1   Mix together all the ingredients except the drumsticks.
2   Remove the skin from the drumsticks and coat them with the tandoori mixture. Leave covered in the fridge for a few hours – preferably overnight.
3   Cook in the oven at 350°F/180°C/gas mark 4 for 25 minutes uncovered and then for 15 minutes covered.
4   Serve with pitta bread and a green salad. When using one drumstick per person, serve with a vegetable curry or bean salad or use as part of a picnic meal.

### Quick Fruit Crumble

SERVES 4
½ teacup porridge oats
½ teacup wholemeal flour
1 rounded tablespoon raw cane sugar
3 tablespoons oil
12 oz (350 g) apricots, stones removed and 4 oz (125 g) young
   marrow, peeled, centre removed, or 1 lb (500 g) fruit in season
Sugar or powdered artificial sweetener to sweeten fruit

1   Pre-heat the oven to 375°F/190°C/gas mark 5.
2   Mix the oats, flour and sugar in a mixing bowl. Pour the oil evenly over the mixture and stir well.
3   If the apricots are firm, partly cook by simmering in a little water. Alternatively, use a microwave for this – follow the instruction booklet for your particular model.
4   Chop the marrow and add to the apricots in a medium-sized ovenproof dish. Sweeten to taste with sugar or artificial sweetener.
5   Place the crumble mixture on top of the fruit and cook for about 35 minutes in the oven until the fruit is cooked and the topping is browned and crispy.

Some fruits may not require sweetening and generally soft fruits do not need to be pre-cooked before baking in the oven. The dish can be divided and cooked in two small containers, allowing one crumble to be frozen for future use.

## Marinated Chicken Casserole
SERVES 2
2 chicken joints
2 tablespoons red wine
1 teaspoon soy sauce
1 teaspoon tomato ketchup
1 clove garlic, crushed
1 small onion, chopped
  Pepper
7 oz (200 g) vegetables, sliced and chopped (e.g. tomato, carrot, celery, courgette, pepper, aubergine)
$\frac{1}{4}$ packet bread sauce mix (if dish is baked in the oven)

1   Trim the chicken of excess fat and skin.
2   Mix the wine, soy sauce, ketchup and garlic together.
3   Place the chicken and onion in a casserole dish and cover with the sauce. Season with pepper. Cover and leave to marinate in the fridge overnight.
4   Add the vegetables to the casserole, arranging the chicken on the top, and bake, covered, at 325°F/170°C/gas mark 3 for at least $1\frac{1}{2}$ hours until the chicken is tender and the vegetables soft.

Alternatively, cook in the microwave, following the instruction booklet for your particular model. Check that the chicken is cooked by piercing it with a skewer. The juices that escape should be clear and not tinged with blood. If necessary, cook for a little longer.

5   If the dish is cooked in the oven, 30 minutes before serving remove the lid, sprinkle on the bread sauce mix and raise the oven temperature a little.

6   Serve with baked or boiled potatoes.

This dish can be frozen before the addition of the bread sauce mix. When reheating, add the sauce mix as a topping. For a change the casserole can be baked with a topping of sliced potatoes, brushed with milk. The chicken is also nice cold with salad.

# 3  COOKING FOR ONE OR TWO

Once the family has grown up and left home, it's all too easy to neglect sensible meals. It needs some ingenuity to keep up the variety and interest without spending a disproportionate amount of time preparing food.

## General Tips

- Try to base two or more meals on one ingredient but prepared in different ways (see 'Variety from the Same Ingredients' on page 33).
- Preparing enough for two days is another sensible practice. Either freeze one or two portions or serve the dish cold or with a slight variation the next day. For example, make a casserole in the oven with a baked potato one day, and the following day reheat the casserole and serve with brown rice or pitta bread.
- A lot of the work when preparing a meal is in assembling the utensils and clearing up afterwards. To save time on this, do some preparation in bulk, such as cleaning enough root vegetables for two days. Store the remainder in the fridge in an airtight bag to prevent browning. Grated cheese can be stored in a jam jar in the fridge for at least a week – no need to grate it each time it is required. It is easier to wash salad items and fruit all in one go. Be careful to handle them lightly and dry well, or the

extra moisture or any bruising will cause decay.

- When buying enough for several days, hygiene is important. First check that the food is very fresh – that is, with a maximum time to the sell-by date. Then, when reheating foods, make sure that they are thoroughly heated through. Never mix raw meat, fish and eggs with a cooked dish. Food should not be reheated more than once.

- It is easy to miss out on using the oven when catering for only one or two. This is a pity, for baked foods have such a special taste and smell. To make using the oven worthwhile, plan a range of dishes to be cooked together. For example, cook a casserole with a braised vegetable, baked potatoes and baked apples along with baked herrings and a baked milk pudding for the next day. Some garlic bread or bread rolls can also be warmed and crisped in the oven just prior to the meal.

- Different vegetables can be boiled in one pot. Remember to start the ones that take longest first. If you want the vegetables separated, wrap them in little bags of aluminium foil. Alternatively, steam vegetables in a sieve or colander over another boiling dish, with a lid on top.

- The old favourite the pressure cooker is not only useful for cooking different vegetables at once, but also for cooking whole meals when catering for small numbers. The avoidance of numerous pots and pans to wash needs to be remembered too.

- Sharing meals with neighbours economizes on effort as well as being more fun.


## Suitable Foods for One or Two

- Individual portions of meat, for example chops,

chicken pieces, pork and gammon steaks.[†]
- Cooked meat, for instance lean ham and tongue.[†]
- Fresh or frozen fish – whole herrings, sardines, mackerel or fish steaks or fillets such as haddock, cod, smoked mackerel or kipper.[†]
- Tinned fish.
- Omelette.
- Stir-fry vegetables – these are especially nice when cooked quickly in small quantities (see page 38).
- Vegetables for stuffing, for example pepper, potato, tomato, avocado.
- Tomato purée in tubes – saves opening a whole tin of tomatoes or purée. Store the opened tube in the fridge.
- Dried fruits, such as apricots, prunes and so on, for a fruit compote.
- Most fruits, such as grapefruit, banana, Ogen melon, peaches, for eating fresh or using in recipes.

## Precautions

When reducing the quantities used in recipes, check the dish earlier than the recommended cooking time, as smaller quantities can cook more quickly.

Pastries, cakes, baked puddings and dishes requiring several stages in preparation can be a lot of work for small numbers. But take heart! These tend to be the less healthy foods anyway. However, it can be worthwhile making quiches or savoury flans if you have a freezer and can freeze individual slices. Alternatively, individual flans can be made in foil cases and the spare ones frozen.

[†] Remember that smoked and tinned fish, ham, gammon and processed cooked meats are all high in salt, so are best used only now and again.

# Variety from the same ingredients

| | |
|---|---|
| White cabbage | Lightly boiled. |
| | Shredded in a coleslaw (see page 90). |
| | Larger outer leaves stuffed with a spicy mince mixture. |
| | Braised with a little olive oil, vinegar, dash of brown sugar, salt and pepper and a little water or stock. |
| Large carton natural yogurt | Spooned over a casserole or a curry as the meal is served. |
| | For tandoori chicken (see page 27). |
| | In a cucumber raita (see page 54). |
| | Added to soup as it is served. |
| | In a syllabub (see page 61) or a reduced-fat cheesecake (see page 113). |
| | Served with fruit. |
| | To make a salad dressing for a coleslaw (see page 90) or a sandwich filling. |
| Whole chicken | Remove raw legs for tandoori chicken (see page 27). |
| | Remove raw wings for soup. |
| | Roast and stuff the remainder with herbs, garlic and citrus fruit juice. |
| | Use any left-over meat in soup or in an open sandwich with a low-calorie mayonnaise, sliced tomatoes, radish and crisp lettuce. |
| Celery | Braised in the oven with stock and grated orange. |
| | In a stew or casserole. |
| | In a salad with apple, nuts, raisins and dressing. |
| | As a crisp stick with a ploughman's lunch. |
| Pitta bread (preferably wholemeal) | Warmed as an accompaniment to a stew or curry. |
| | Stuffed with fish or cheese filling for a snack meal, starter or picnic (see page 98). |
| | Used as a base for a pizza (see page 73). |
| | Used in strips along with vegetable sticks as an accompaniment to a cheese, nut, fish or vegetable dip (see pages 97, 110). |

## The Freezer

A freezer can be a great asset to successful catering for small numbers. A fridge-freezer may be all that is required, however. Large freezers are useful for frequent entertaining and storing home-grown fruits and vegetables and home-baked bread.

*Advantages*

- A freezer allows you to cook for four or more with all the benefits of economy of scale, as spare portions can be frozen for another day. This means that there is no need to eat the same dish on consecutive days.
- Strawberries and raspberries can be frozen and then small quantities used as a basis for a fruit salad or a compote as required.
- Beans such as haricot, pinto or kidney can be cooked in bulk and frozen in small containers.
- The uncooked topping for fruit crumble and fresh breadcrumbs both store well in the freezer, allowing them to be prepared in bulk.
- Ice cream can be stored – a good standby for entertaining the family.
- Ready-frozen vegetables can be stored, which can be convenient, particularly when fresh ones are expensive. There is no waste and when using frozen vegetables it is easy to serve small quantities of different coloured vegetables at the same meal – making meals more interesting.
- Family-sized packs of food can be bought, in the knowledge that part can be frozen until required, for example large loaves or bread rolls.
- Food reduced for quick sale can be bought for freezing. Do not forget that once defrosted it must be eaten immediately.

- Entertaining can be so tiring, particularly if you are out of regular practice in cooking for large numbers. A freezer can help to alleviate the strain as the main dishes can be cooked in advance. A microwave can be invaluable for reheating. However, when reheating with a microwave check the whole dish is heated through as you can get cold spots.

*Dos and Don'ts with the Freezer*
- Label items clearly with their name and the date of freezing, and store your home-made meat and fish dishes for no more than three months.
- For manufactured foods carefully read the storage details for the 'star rating' on your freezer.
- If uncooked frozen foods accidentally defrost, cook them as soon as possible, then they can be quickly refrozen. But otherwise never refreeze foods.
- Make sure that everything is very well sealed as freezers, like fridges, dehydrate food.
- Always allow plenty of time for complete defrosting, particularly with poultry. If you are in any doubt, put a skewer into the food and check that it is soft right through – this is where a microwave can be useful as it will defrost food in a fraction of the usual time.

## The Microwave Oven

As with most new gadgets it takes time to adapt to a microwave. It can, however, be a great asset as long as you are not expecting the answer to all your cooking needs.

Microwaves have a number of uses:

- A traditional oven uses the same amount of fuel regardless of the number of dishes in it. In a microwave, cooking time roughly halves as you halve the quantities. It is therefore very practical for small portions.
- A microwave will reheat pre-prepared meals – particularly useful if you cook for a freezer. It will defrost food and reheat it in the container in which it was frozen (provided there is no metal in the container – so avoid aluminium foil). It also allows for last-minute changes. For example, an extra loaf from the freezer can be defrosted when the family unexpectedly arrives for tea.
- A microwave simplifies the preparation of some dishes such as white sauce, scrambled eggs, quick savoury mince and casseroles.
- Milk is heated easily, as are half-drunk cups of tea and coffee, which is useful if you find that forgetfulness or frequent distracting phone calls are a problem. It is also worth noting that a microwave works only for the time you have programmed it, avoiding the risk of accidentally leaving food to burn and boil dry.
- Foods boiled in water take as long in a microwave as on a hob. However, cooking food, especially vegetables, in just a few tablespoons of water, rather like steaming, gives a good result.
- Healthy low-fat cooking is easier in a microwave. Because the heat does not come from the bottom of the container as on a conventional hob, foods less readily stick and burn in the absence of fat.
- On busy days, ready-prepared meals can be left plated in the fridge. When you arrive home tired and hungry they can simply be reheated on the plate. Similarly, if you are disturbed during your meal, it can easily be rewarmed.

For people reliant on meals-on-wheels or meals prepared by a relative, a microwave can be invaluable. However, it can be too difficult to learn how to use a new gadget at this late stage in life. It is, therefore, sound sense to be prepared by getting accustomed to this useful machine, early in retirement when cooking itself is still enjoyed.

*Shortcomings*
You cannot beat your traditional hob or oven for browning food such as meat or pastry or for the flavour they impart. It may be necessary to buy new plastic and glass dishes as metal pans and containers cannot be used in the microwave.

# Recipes

*Stuffed Avocado*
SERVES 2
1 large or 2 small ripe avocados
2 dessertspoons lemon juice
2 tablespoons fromage frais
2 teaspoons low-calorie mayonnaise *or* salad cream
$\frac{1}{2}$ stick celery, finely chopped
$\frac{1}{4}$ apple, diced
1 tablespoon chopped green pepper
1 tablespoon chopped walnuts or cashew nuts
1 dessertspoon chopped fresh herbs, if available
$\frac{1}{2}$ slice lean ham, diced, *or* 1 tablespoon peeled prawns, thawed if frozen.

1   Wash the avocado, slice in half lengthways and remove the stone.
2   Spoon the lemon juice over each half.
3   Mix the remaining ingredients together, retaining two nuts and two pieces of ham or two prawns for garnishing. Pile the mixture into the avocado and garnish.
4   Serve with warmed brown French stick or hot granary or wholemeal rolls.

When used for a starter rather than a light meal, this mixture will serve four people using two avocados.

*Stir-fry Vegetables with Nuts*

SERVES 2
2 tablespoons oil
1 clove garlic
1 medium onion, sliced
2 teaspoons fresh root ginger, finely chopped
10–12 oz (300–350 g) mixed vegetables, e.g. small sticks of carrot, celery, leek, red or green pepper or courgette; small cauliflower or broccoli florets; sliced mushrooms or bean sprouts
1 tablespoon soy sauce
Black pepper, freshly ground
2 oz (50 g) cashew nuts

1  Heat the oil and fry the garlic and onion in it briskly for 2–3 minutes, then add the ginger and cook for a further 2 minutes.
2  Add the hard vegetables that require longest cooking – the carrot, celery or cauliflower. Continue to fry quickly for about 5 minutes, turning the vegetables frequently so that they do not stick to the pan and burn.
3  Next add the vegetables that take a moderate time to cook, such as courgette, broccoli or pepper. Continue cooking for 3 minutes.
4  Finally add the quick-cooking vegetables, like mushrooms and beansprouts, and fry for 2 minutes. Stir in the soy sauce and black pepper. Cook for a further 3 minutes or until vegetables are sufficiently cooked: they should still retain some crispness.

5   Stir in the nuts and serve immediately accompanied by warmed and crisped granary bread stick.

## Grilled Egg au Gratin

SERVES 1

1 tablespoon milk
$\frac{1}{2}$ tomato, thinly sliced
1 egg
  Salt and pepper
$\frac{1}{2}$ (15 g) reduced-fat Cheddar cheese, grated

1   Heat a small, fireproof dish such as a ramekin by immersing it in hot water or, if the oven is on, heat it for a few minutes in the oven. Grease the dish well.
2   Put the milk and tomato slices in the dish and break the egg on top.
3   Season with pepper and lightly with salt if required. Sprinkle the cheese on top.
4   Cook under a very low grill for 25–30 minutes until the egg is set.
5   Serve with wholemeal bread.

## Meat Loaf

SERVES 4–6

  2 slices of wholemeal bread
12 oz (350 g) extra-lean minced beef
$\frac{1}{2}$ teaspoon mixed herbs
2–3 oz (50–75 g) gammon offcuts, trimmed of fat, *or* 1 gammon
      steak (from a packet of 2)
  1 medium onion, chopped
  1 clove garlic, crushed
  1 egg
  3 tablespoons stock *or* water
    Pinch of mixed spice
$\frac{1}{4}$ teaspoon salt
    Pepper
    Oil for greasing
  2 bay leaves

1   Make the bread into crumbs in a food grinder or processor, or with a hand grater. Add to the beef and mixed herbs in a bowl.

2   Chop the gammon and liquidize with the onion, garlic, egg, stock or water, spice, salt and pepper. Alternatively, mix all these ingredients together by hand very thoroughly.

3   Combine with the other ingredients in the bowl.

4   Grease a small pudding basin or soufflé dish of at least 1¼ pint (750 ml) capacity. Place the bay leaves on the bottom and then add the mixture and press down firmly

5   Cover with aluminium foil and steam for 2½ hours until cooked right through. Regularly check that the saucepan is not boiling dry and top up with boiling water if necessary. Alternatively, bake in a loaf tin in the oven at 350°F/180°C/gas mark 4 for about 50 minutes.

6   Serve hot with cooked vegetables, cold with a salad or sliced in a sandwich with mustard and lettuce.

# 4 A TASTE OF HEALTH

The foods which are valuable for preventing nutritional deficiency and ill health in later life are considered in an earlier chapter, 'Basic Nutrition Know-how' (see page 3). This chapter is concerned with the most common diet-related illnesses. These are due to an over-consumption of energy (calories), fat (especially saturated fat), sugar and salt, and to taking too few of the fibre-rich foods. So how do these elements of the diet affect health?

## Energy

Becoming overweight by storing a surplus of energy (calories) as body fat puts a strain on the heart, lungs, circulation, bones and joints. Carrying excess weight increases the risk of heart disease, high blood pressure and strokes, and aggravates complaints like arthritis.

Fat and sugar provide energy in a concentrated form. It is therefore easy to over-eat when there is a lot of them in the food you choose.

## Fat

Although too much fat of any kind can affect health by causing excess weight, it is the saturated fat particularly that should be taken only in small quantities. Too much saturated fat raises the cholesterol level in the blood.

The cholesterol can then be deposited on the artery walls and this can lead to a blockage and heart disease. Eating too much fat has also been linked to breast and colon cancers and gall bladder disease.

## Sugar

Apart from leading to overweight, sugar encourages tooth decay and gum disease. It also provides empty calories – that is, just energy without valuable nutrients. So generally sugar is a poor choice of food in later life when the appetite is reduced. Other more nutritious foods can provide all the energy that is required. When a high proportion of the diet's energy comes from sugar, ill health can result from a deficiency of important nutrients.

## Salt

Present evidence suggests that too much salt in the diet leads to raised blood pressure (hypertension). This increases the likelihood of a stroke. We do know that some people are more prone to hypertension than others and this tendency can run in families. Most of us can recall friends and relatives who enjoyed a long and healthy life in spite of a high salt intake. However when whole nations are compared, there is evidence of a link between a country's salt intake and their incidence of hypertension and strokes – a higher salt intake resulting in more strokes. Taking care over the amount of salt you use is especially important if you or your relatives suffer from hypertension, but it is still sensible advice for us all. After all it is difficult for individuals to know whether they are at particular risk.

## Fibre

Fibre is another word for roughage, the part of food not absorbed by the body. It helps food pass quickly and easily through the body, reducing the risk of digestive disorders such as diverticular disease and piles. It also helps to prevent the common and unpleasant complaint of constipation.

Foods high in fibre are also rich in valuable nutrients. Eating a diet full of fibre-rich foods and with little fat and sugar therefore helps to prevent unnecessary tiredness, poor healing and lowered resistance to infection.

## Sources of Advice

Well-researched reports about food and health have been published by the Government, Health Education Council (now the Health Education Authority), British Medical Association and World Health Organization since 1983. These have formed the basis of the current advice on healthy eating. However, the Government feels that clear evidence about the link between sugar and health is still lacking, and, therefore, in 1987 a new working party was convened to examine the effect of sugar in the diet, the findings of which were not available at the time of writing this book.

How to eat healthily by using less sugar and salt is considered below. Practical advice on eating well, with less fat and more fibre, is provided in the following two chapters.

## The Natural Flavour of Food

Some sugar and salt is naturally present in food. But most of the sugar and salt in our diet has been added to food. By eating food with less added sugar and salt you can relearn the pleasures of the natural flavours of food.

*Sugar in the Diet*
The most common sources of sugar in the diet are:
  Sugar spooned into drinks and used in cooking.
  Cakes and biscuits.
  Sweets and chocolates.
  Desserts.
  Soft and alcoholic drinks.
  Preserves, pickles and honey.
  Tinned fruit in syrup.
  Processed foods.

Read the ingredients list on the packaging of processed foods. How many products can you find without added sugar? Apart from the word 'sugar', look out for words ending in '-ose', like 'maltose' and 'glucose', which are types of sugar. 'Syrup', 'honey' or 'molasses' on an ingredients list also mean that sugars have been added. You will probably be surprised at how many savoury foods have some form of sugar added.

EATING LESS SUGAR
- Use fruit as the basis of most of your desserts. Fruit contains natural sweetness, so there is rarely need to add sugar. For sour fruit like rhubarb a little grated orange rind or the addition, after cooking, of some orange juice can reduce tartness and the amount of sugar required for sweetening.
- Home-made scones, tea-breads and griddle cakes only need a little sugar. Dried fruit and fruit juice can be added for sweetening. These make healthy alternatives to most bought cakes and biscuits.
- Fruit canned in natural juice makes an excellent

base for fruit salad. It has more flavour and contains less sugar than fruit in syrup.

- Generally look out for reduced-sugar products or ones without added sugar, such as certain baked beans, fruit yogurts and soft drinks.
- Choose dry alcoholic drinks in preference to sweet ones.
- If you are a sweet or chocolate nibbler, try to satisfy this urge with a little fresh or dried fruit or raw carrots instead.
- Artificial sweeteners can be helpful. If saccharin leaves you with an after-taste, try instead a product containing aspartame (Nutrasweet) or acesulfame k (Sunett), such as Canderel, Hermestas Gold, Sweet N'Low or Diamin.
- A banana sandwich, made with wholemeal bread spread with a little low-fat soft cheese in place of a spreading fat, can satisfy the desire for something sweet and filling – a suitable teatime snack.
- If you have a sweet tooth, gradually adjust yourself to fewer sweetened foods. Little by little reduce the sugar in recipes and if you add sugar in drinks, just cut down by half a teaspoon at first. Don't expect to adapt immediately, but given time you will probably grow to dislike very sweet foods. How often have you heard people say, 'I can't understand how I used to drink my tea with sugar!'?

*Salt in the Diet*
The most common sources of salt in the diet are:
  Salt added in cooking and at table.
  Processed fish, for example smoked, salted.
  Processed meat, for instance salami, sausages, burgers, pies and tinned meat.
  Most cheeses.
  Stock cubes, meat and yeast extracts.

Tinned and packet soups.
Bread, biscuits.
Most breakfast cereals.
Crisps, salted nuts and savoury biscuits.

When reading the ingredients list on packaged food, look out for the words 'sodium chloride' and 'brine' as these are other terms for salt. At least a third of our salt comes from cereal products, including bread. If your doctor has suggested a low-salt diet, take particular care over the bread you eat. In this circumstance try to find a baker who will make a low-salt or salt-free bread; otherwise consider making your own.

EATING LESS SALT

- Salt masks the flavour of food. But it may take a little while before you really enjoy the natural flavour of vegetables cooked without salt.
- Make good use of herbs, spices and flavourings:

  Add fresh or dried herbs to meat and fish, for instance mint to lamb; rosemary to chicken, fresh sardines or lamb; sage to chicken and turkey livers or white meat.

  Use orange, lemon or lime juice and their grated rind or vinegar to flavour salads, fish and chicken dishes and curries.

  Nutmeg sprinkled on to vegetables like cauliflower, cabbage, spinach or boiled potato is delicious.

  Try chopped parsley sprinkled over vegetables.

  Add curry spices to meat, fish, bean, lentil and vegetable dishes.

  Use basil, mixed herbs, marjoram or oregano in stews and dishes containing tomatoes.

  Turmeric or cloves boiled with wholemeal rice can give it a lift.

Try ginger with marrow or lightly stir-fried vegetables, or rubbed on to pork or lamb chops.

Mustard rubbed over kidney or chicken before
cooking makes a tasty change.

Black, white or paprika pepper, nutmeg, cumin or
home-made mustard (without added salt) can
replace the salt put on the table.

- Gradually replace meals using ham, bacon, smoked
fish and meat products, like pies and sausages, with
less salty alternatives. Use instead small quantities
of lean fresh meat, fresh or frozen fish and vegetarian meals based on dried beans, lentils or unsalted nuts.

- Many highly flavoured vegetables used in casseroles
provide a distinct taste, allowing less salt to be used.
For example, try using onions, garlic, leeks, aubergines, celery, mushrooms, spinach or peppers.

- Remember that using stock cubes, meat and yeast
extract, powdered soup or certain sauces such as soy
or Worcester is just another way of adding salt.

## What About Alcohol?

Alcohol can stimulate the appetite, enhance the flavour
of food and help relaxation. Nonetheless it should be
used with care. On ageing, the body detoxifies alcohol
less well. Alcohol also provides calories which are
obtained from more nutritious foods. It can be easy to
skip a meal and satisfy the appetite with a few drinks,
but beware: replacing meals with alcohol means you go
short of important nutrients. Similarly, as it is expensive, it can use up money that could otherwise be spent
on valuable foods. It is best not to drink every day, to
give your body at least a day's break from handling this
toxic substance which some studies have shown to be

implicated in a number of health problems. Moderation is the key: for men a sensible limit is about ten drinks per week and for women about six. A drink means $\frac{1}{2}$ pint (300 ml) of ordinary beer or cider, a single measure of spirits, a small glass of sherry, a glass of wine or a wine glass of vintage cider.


## Food Additives

With all the claims on food packaging, such as 'Additive and preservative free' or 'Only natural ingredients used', it is no wonder we consider additives harmful. The whole issue of additives is complicated and influenced by a number of factors.

Additives approved by the European Community are assigned an E number. A few of the additives approved for use in the UK do not have an E number. Additives have a variety of uses in foods, such as: adding colour (the E100 series), preventing rancidity and staling (E300 series), maintaining the texture (E400 series), protecting against food decay and poisoning (E200 series), adding sweetness or enhancing flavour.

Generally, foods with many additives are highly processed and contain a lot of sugar, fat or salt. Such foods also tend to be depleted of fibre and useful minerals and vitamins. Conversely, basic foods that have undergone little processing do not suffer this depletion. It is, therefore, wise to use mainly basic foods for their other qualities and not just because they contain few or no additives. In fact, some approved additives are valuable vitamins and minerals. Would you really turn your nose up at E300, additive 375, E140 and E290 if you knew what they were? E300 is the valuable ascorbic acid, or in other words vitamin C. The UK approved additive 375 is used as a colour or

stabiliser but is in fact a B vitamin. On the other hand you may be looking at some E140 right now and you'll definitely be breathing E290. Have you guessed? Well E140 is the colour chlorophyll from plants and E290 is plain carbon dioxide. All additives have to undergo vigorous testing for their safety. One should not forget that the removal of some other additives from foods could be extremely harmful. For example, food poisoning could result if nitrates and nitrites were removed from cured meats. However some additives such as certain colourings and flavourings can quite safely be removed from products. Many of these additives can be considered superfluous. You may prefer a margarine or butter with a more subtle colour, rather than a brilliant yellow. Similarly a bright orange fruit squash that stains your tongue may not appeal. How ready are you to accept brown raspberries, blackcurrants or tinned peas?

Natural additives are not necessarily better than synthetic ones. Just as the addition of extra fat, sugar and salt to foods can be harmful to health, so too can the addition of 'unnatural' amounts of a natural additive such as a colouring!

You can find out more about food additives by

writing to the Ministry of Agriculture, Fisheries and Food (address on page 117) which produces the free leaflet *Food Additives: The Numbers Identified* and the booklet *Food Additives: The Balanced Approach*.

## Dieting's a Bore

Eating more food of any kind than you need means surplus energy (calories) is stored as fat. That is how weight problems develop. Going on diets and then putting on weight as soon as there is an excuse to eat your guilt-ridden and banned foods is such a bore.

Seriously following advice on healthy eating can do away with the need for dieting. Watching the amount of fat, sugar and alcohol in your everyday diet and eating plenty of the satisfying high-fibre foods is far more fun than dieting. A study in 1984 of around 500 people who were trying to eat a healthier diet containing less fat and sugar and more fibre found that many of them reduced their calorie intake without trying. The high-fibre foods were bulky and filling, compared to the foods they were accustomed to, which were higher in fat and sugar. They therefore felt so full on their new diet that they could not eat their normal amount of calories.

There are many delicious modern alternatives to dishes traditionally high in fat and sugar. Also the occasional fattening but favourite foods, such as a pork pie or fried fish and chips, can still be incorporated into your otherwise healthy diet. Trying to ban foods you really miss is usually a recipe for disaster. You will probably end up eating far more in the end and feel full of guilt.

Aim for a sensible way of eating that maintains a healthy weight, of which the occasional guilt-free treat is an integral part. See page 78 for suggested portion sizes of meat, cheese and other foods.

## Diabetes

Diabetes affects at least one in a hundred of the population and the incidence increases with age. The majority of diabetics are diagnosed from late middle age. Very often the problem is identified by something that appears quite unrelated. This can be a visit to the optician, due to a sudden change in eyesight, treatment by a chiropodist for a foot sore or by a doctor for a skin infection. Other symptoms of untreated diabetes include urinary and lung infections, thirst, tiredness, some loss of weight and passing more urine. Finding sugar in the urine and a raised level of sugar or glucose in the blood helps to confirm the diagnosis. Diabetes which develops later in life (maturity onset diabetes) is far more common among those who are overweight – another reason to try to keep at a healthy weight! Advice to avoid sugar, restrict fat and fill up on the wholegrain and high-fibre foods is particularly valuable in the treatment of this disorder.

If you are entertaining a diabetic, you can cook the same food for everyone. Avoid desserts with added sugar and choose healthy dishes that are high in fibre and low in fat. Potatoes, wholemeal bread and brown rice should be encouraged rather than avoided. Further advice for diabetics is obtainable from the British Diabetic Association (address on page 117).

## Common Misconceptions

Many misunderstandings and myths exist about food and health. Some of the most common ones are explained here.

### 'Cholesterol should be avoided'

It is true that a high level of cholesterol in the blood increases the risk of coronary heart disease. However, most of the cholesterol in the blood is made within the body. Eating saturated fat pushes up the blood cholesterol more than eating the high cholesterol foods. So for health it is therefore the hard and animal fats that need to be restricted. In fact, to save public confusion margarine can only be advertised as low in cholesterol or cholesterol-free if it is also high in polyunsaturated fats and low in saturated ones.

### 'Sugar is needed for energy'

All food provides energy. The body's sugar is released into the blood as it is needed. As explained before, sugar provides no valuable nutrients. The truth is that eating more nourishing foods makes you feel far more energetic.

### 'Bran is good for us'

Bran, found in the outer layer of cereals, is rich in fibre and therefore does prevent constipation and other disorders of the bowel. However, by eating plenty of the wholegrain cereals and breads, vegetables and fruits, you can get all the fibre you need. Pure bran does not provide all the nutrients contained in wholesome wholegrain foods such as many B vitamins, iron and other minerals. Adding bran to the diet can also cause malabsorption of valuable minerals.

### 'Meat makes a meal'

Meat is a good source of valuable iron and protein. However, vegetarians tend to be healthier than meat-eaters, having a lower incidence of many diet-related diseases. They obtain iron from other foods such as those listed on page 7. Sufficient protein is easily provided by eggs, cheese, milk, yogurt, nuts, pulses and cereals.

## 'Some foods slim you down'

No foods slim you down as such. Nonetheless ideas about the slimming properties of foods such as grapefruit do exist. The only known fact is that some foods help you to keep a good figure as they are less fattening than their alternatives. For example vegetables, fruits, and wholemeal bread are filling and can replace excess meat and cheese, biscuits, chocolates and puddings.

## 'Bread and potatoes are fattening'

At one time slimmers believed that potatoes, bread and starchy foods were the ones to avoid. In fact sugar, fat and alcohol are more fattening than starchy foods. It is the fat and sugar eaten with bread, potatoes and cereals that need the care. For example jam and butter or margarine are spread on bread and potatoes are often buttered or cooked with fat. A 'harmless' bread dough can be fried and dipped in sugar and turned into a doughnut. It is worth remembering that just 1 oz (25 g) of butter or margarine is as fattening as three medium slices of filling wholemeal bread or nearly 10 oz (300 g) of boiled potatoes.

We are now appreciating the full benefit of plain potatoes, wholewheat breads and pastas, wholegrain rice and cereals (without added sugar). These foods which are full of valuable vitamins, minerals and fibre are also filling. It's much more difficult to overeat when feeling satisfied with a good plateful of boiled or baked potatoes or other starchy foods. Slimmers take note: cutting back on just the bread and potatoes can actually lead to weight problems. More fattening meat, cheese and biscuits can readily take their place. This also pushes up the proportion of fat in the diet and increases the risk of heart disease and constipation.

*'Doesn't matter what I eat as I don't gain weight'*
If you are slim it is easy to believe you must be eating well. Eating a sensible diet, low in fatty and sugary foods, is usually the reason for being a healthy weight. However, this isn't always the case.

To keep you at the right weight the energy you receive from food should be just enough for the body to function and for all the daily activities. A diet chosen from foods of poor nutritional quality can provide the right amount of energy but be short of necessary nutrients. Whatever your weight, the quality of food is important. Slim people can still suffer from complaints such as anaemia, weak bones, constipation and a build up of fats in the arteries. So they too should avoid obtaining a high proportion of their energy from fat and sugar.

## Recipes

### Cucumber Raita
SERVES 4
3 in. (7.5 cm) piece of cucumber, diced
1 clove garlic, crushed
4 tablespoons thick set natural yogurt
$\frac{1}{4}$ teaspoon salt
$\frac{1}{2}$ teaspoon dried mint *or* 1 dessertspoon finely chopped fresh mint
Pinch of cayenne pepper

1 Mix all the ingredients together except the cayenne.
2 Sprinkle the cayenne lightly on top.
3 Chill before serving.

This is delightful with curries or salads. Alternatively, it can be served as a starter with wholemeal pitta bread.

54

## Crab Salad

SERVES 4 AS A STARTER OR 2–3 AS A LIGHT MEAL

½ apple, cored
½ stick celery
6 oz (175 g) fresh or tinned crab meat
4 tablespoons natural yogurt
2 tablespoons low-calorie mayonnaise
1 tablespoon lemon juice
1 teaspoon curry powder
  Crisp lettuce leaves
  Paprika pepper
4 rings green pepper
4 walnuts

1  Halve the apple lengthways and then slice the two pieces widthways. Cut the celery into three lengthways and slice finely.
2  Mix the prepared apple and celery with the crab meat, yogurt, mayonnaise, lemon juice and curry powder.
3  Divide the crab mixture between individual beds of crisp lettuce.
4  Garnish each serving with a sprinkling of paprika pepper, a ring of green pepper and a walnut.
5  Serve with dark rye bread or warmed pitta bread.

## Apricot Fluff

SERVES 4

8 oz (250 g) apricots
  Artificial sweetener or brown sugar
1 egg white
3 rounded tablespoons fromage frais
2 rounded tablespoons natural yogurt
2 tablespoons crunchy cereal.

1  Peel and stone the apricots and simmer gently until soft in 1–2 tablespoons water, or cook without water in a microwave. Sweeten to taste and beat to a smooth pulp. Allow to cool.
2  Beat the egg white until stiff but not dry.
3  Mix the fromage frais and yogurt with the cooled apricots, then fold in the beaten egg white.
4  Pour into four wine glasses and top with the crunchy cereal. Chill before serving.

This dessert keeps well for a day in the fridge, making it suitable for serving two portions on consecutive days. Fresh apricots can be replaced with tinned ones – these need to be liquidized in 1 tablespoon of their juice.

# 5  FLAVOUR WITHOUT FAT

## Fat in the Diet

The most common sources of fat in the diet are:

Full-fat milk, cream.
Full-fat hard and soft cheeses.
Cooking and spreading fats – butter, lard, suet, oil, margarine.
Meat and meat products: pies, pâté, sausages, burgers.
Cakes, biscuits, pastries, confectionery.
Fried foods, including chips.

Most of the main sources of fat in the diet provide fat in a saturated form (which, as has already been explained, should be taken only in small quantities). Polyunsaturated fat, a form of unsaturated fat, is found in corn, soya, sunflower, safflower and grapeseed oils. The polyunsaturated fats tend to be soft or liquid at room temperature, whereas the saturated ones are hard. Some soft margarines are made from oils rich in polyunsaturated fat and these are preferable to ones consisting of the harder, more saturated fats – always check the details on the packet. Don't, however, be fooled into believing that the polyunsaturated fats are slimming – a common misunderstanding. In fact they are just as fattening as the saturated ones, so they should still be used sparingly. Generally, animal fats are of the saturated, hard kind. However, do not be misled by terms like 'non-animal fat': vegetable fat can be hydrogenated, making it harder and more saturated, such as that found in ice cream or biscuits. Also coconut and palm oils, although 'non-animal fat', contain a lot of saturated fat.

*Using Less Fat*
- Substitute some of the following foods for their higher-fat alternatives:

    Semi-skimmed or skimmed milk.
    Natural yogurt, low-fat soft cheeses.
    Reduced-fat hard cheeses.
    Edam, Gouda and other medium-fat cheeses.
    Liver, kidney, lean red meat and lean pork.
    Poultry (skin removed), rabbit.
    Lean mince, reduced-fat sausages and pâtés.
    Home-made wholemeal scones and tea-breads, using just a little polyunsaturated oil or margarine.
    Fish – fresh or tinned, drained of oil.

- Use a non-stick frying pan and brown meat and vegetables in their own juices.
- Drain off fat when cooking meat such as when roasting, grilling or making a casserole. Where possible, let the fat settle on stews, casseroles and gravies and then skim it off.
- Use flavoursome vegetables, herbs, spices and flavourings to allow for any loss in flavour when cooking with less fat. For example, instead of frying fish, grill it with herbs, lemon juice and garlic. A good alternative is to bake it with tomatoes, onions, herbs and peppers. Also try some of the suggestions on page 46 for flavouring food in a 'healthy' way.
- Adding crisp vegetables such as celery to casseroles to help compensate for eating fewer crispy fried foods. As an alternative, serve crisp salad vegetables

such as chicory or lettuce. Adding a few nuts or seeds and serving warm and crisped bread rolls or crusty French bread also provides a crunchy texture at a meal.

- When you do need a little fat in cooking, preferably use a corn, soya, sunflower, safflower or grapeseed oil; otherwise select a margarine high in poly-unsaturates.

- Try to eat bread continental-style, without butter. You are less likely to miss the butter when choosing different varieties of bread, with interesting shapes and textures.

- When using less fat, more starchy foods like potatoes, pasta and bread are needed at each meal to satisfy the appetite.

- When eating snacks on toast there is no need to butter the toast. To compensate for any loss in flavour add mixed herbs to scrambled eggs, tomatoes or sliced peppers to cheese and fish on toast, or curry powder to baked beans.

- Try introducing a few cooked beans to casseroles, to reduce the quantity of meat required and therefore the amount of fat eaten.

## Recipes

*Creamy Pasta*

SERVES 2

4 oz (125 g) wholewheat *or* green spaghetti
$\frac{1}{2}$ tablespoon oil
1 clove garlic, crushed
1 small onion, finely chopped
1 × 7 oz (200 g) tin tomatoes, drained and chopped
$\frac{1}{4}$ red or green pepper, diced
4 oz (125 g) fromage frais
4 oz (125 g) natural yogurt

Pinch of dried thyme *or* ½ tablespoon fresh thyme
2 teaspoons tomato ketchup
Black pepper and salt
1 oz (25 g) nuts, e.g. cashews, walnuts, chopped (optional)

1   Boil the spaghetti in 2 pints (1 litre) water for 20 minutes (less if using green spaghetti), until just cooked.
2   Heat the oil and lightly fry the garlic and onion for about 5 minutes.
3   Add the tomatoes and the pepper. Simmer for about 10 minutes, until the onion and pepper are soft.
4   Remove from the heat and stir in the fromage frais, yogurt, thyme and ketchup. Warm through, but do not boil. Season to taste with salt and pepper.
5   Serve the pasta sprinkled with freshly ground black pepper and covered with the sauce. If using the nuts, scatter them on the top.
6   Prepare a green salad or spinach as an accompaniment.

If you are able to buy only a 14 oz (400 g) tin of tomatoes, use half in this recipe and save the remainder with all the juice to make the vegetable and nut loaf (see page 98) or add them to a casserole.

## *Pork with Apricots*

SERVES 2
2 oz (50 g) dried apricots
4 fl oz (125 ml) boiling water
1 tablespoon oil
1 medium onion, sliced
2 sticks of celery, sliced
8 oz (250 g) pork steak, trimmed and diced
2 teaspoons curry powder
½ chicken stock cube dissolved in 4 fl oz (125 ml) boiling water
2 tablespoons natural yogurt

1   Soak the apricots in the boiling water for at least 15 minutes.
2   Heat the oil and fry the onion and celery for 3 minutes. Add the pork and fry till brown on all sides. Sprinkle on the curry powder.
3   Add the stock to the pan with the apricots.

4   Cover and simmer for 25–30 minutes until the pork and vegetables are tender.
5   Remove from the heat and stir in the yogurt.
6   Serve with brown rice or baked potatoes and a green vegetable.

## *Lemon Syllabub*

SERVES 2
   Grated rind and juice of ¼ lemon
4 oz (125 g) low-fat fromage frais
4 oz (125 g) low-fat yogurt
1 rounded teaspoon soft brown sugar
1 desertspoon sherry
   Roasted flaked almonds *or* sunflower seeds

1   Mix all the ingredients together, except the nuts or seeds.
2   Divide between two wine glasses. Sprinkle the nuts or seeds on top and chill.
3   Serve with a wholemeal biscuit – preferably home-made.


Careful use has been made of fat throughout the recipes. However, for the benefit of those choosing a low-fat diet, the following recipes are notably low in fat: tandoori chicken (page 27), meat loaf (page 39), cucumber raita (page 54), crab salad (page 55), apricot fluff (page 55), corn and potato soup (page 64), chicken liver and vegetable hot pot (page 75), spaghetti with tomato lentil bolognaise (page 80), stuffed pitta (page 98), date and apple tea-bread (page 105).

# 6 FIBRE-RICH FOOD

## How Much Fibre?

A suitable target for good health is about 1 oz (25 g) of fibre per day. Younger and more active people may easily eat more.

## Daily Sources of Fibre

Fibre is found in wholegrain cereals, fruit and vegetables – including peas, beans and lentils. The fibre content of many important sources of dietary fibre is given below to help you check the amount in your diet. You may find it necessary to eat a little extra bread or breakfast cereal. This may need to be balanced by using a lower-fat milk, eating less butter or having fewer biscuits and sweets. It may be sufficient simply to eat more vegetables and from time to time to substitute a few beans for some meat.

| Fibre Content (Grams) | Food | Portion Size |
|---|---|---|
| 7.5 | Haricot and kidney beans, cooked | 1 portion of 3½ oz (100 g) |
| 7.5 | Baked beans | ½ small tin |
| 7.0 | Peas, boiled | 1 small portion of 2 oz (50 g) |
| 5.0 | Wholewheat pasta, e.g. spaghetti | 1 serving – nearly 2 oz (50 g) uncooked weight |
| 4.0 | Wholewheat breakfast biscuits | 2 biscuits |
| 4.0 | Muesli | 1 bowl of 2 oz (50 g) |
| 3.5 | Lentils, boiled | 1 small serving of 3½ oz (100 g) – 1 oz (25 g) uncooked weight |

| 3.0 | Wholemeal bread | 1 medium slice from a large cut loaf |
| 3.0 | Wholemeal scone | 1 × 2 oz (50 g) scone |
| 3.0 | Vegetables, e.g. spring greens, Brussels sprouts, cabbage, carrots, cauliflower | 1 serving of $3\frac{1}{2}$ oz (100 g) |
| 3.0 | Banana | 1 medium-sized fruit |
| 3.0 | Boiled new potatoes | 1 medium portion of 5–6 oz (150–175 g) |
| 2.5 | Apple or pear, unpeeled | 1 fruit |
| 2.5 | Peanuts | A handful – about 1 oz (25 g) |
| 2.0 | Orange | 1 fruit |
| 2.0 | Brown rice | 1 serving – nearly 2 oz (50 g) uncooked weight |
| 2.0 | Dried fruit, e.g. currants, raisins | A good handful – about 1 oz (25 g) |
| 2.0 | Rye crispbread | 2 biscuits |
| 1.5 | Porridge | 1 bowl of 6 oz (175 g) |
| 1.5 | Cornflakes | 1 small bowl of $\frac{1}{2}$ oz (15 g) |
| 1.5 | Salad, mixed, e.g. tomato, lettuce, cucumber, beetroot, radish | A good portion of 3 oz (75 g) |
| 1.0 | White bread | 1 thin slice from a large loaf |
| 0.5 | Digestive biscuits | 1 small biscuit |

## Increasing Your Fibre Intake

- Try to substitute wholemeal bread and flour, brown rice and wholewheat pasta for the white varieties.
- Fine self-raising wholemeal flour can give excellent results. But if you are still disappointed when baking with wholemeal flour, then try using half white flour, or an extra flat teaspoonful of baking powder per 8 oz/225 g of wholemeal flour.
- High-fibre foods need to be increased gradually to save unnecessary indigestion. However, you may find some high-fibre foods need to be avoided as they simply don't suit you.
- Wholegrain products absorb more moisture so be prepared for this when cooking. For instance, when making wholemeal cakes or boiling brown rice or

pasta, a little more liquid is required. It is also important to drink more fluid yourself.

- Brown rice takes about 10–15 minutes longer than white to cook and wholewheat pasta takes at least 5 minutes longer than white.

- Wholegrain foods have a stronger, nuttier taste, so once you are used to them, the white products may seem rather boring.

- It may be helpful to plan meals around the rice, pasta, bread or potatoes (the starchy foods) as well as around the other vegetables. This contrasts with our traditional method of centring the meal on meat or fish. It is almost a reversal of our current thinking – having the meat, fish or cheese more as an accompaniment!

## Recipes

*Corn and Potato Soup*
SERVES 4
2 small onions, chopped

1 large potato, roughly diced
1 pint (600 ml) chicken stock
  Black pepper and salt
1 × 11½ oz (335 g) tin sweetcorn, drained
5 fl oz (150 ml) semi-skimmed milk
½ teaspoon dried thyme

1   Place the onions and potato in a pan with the chicken stock. Cover and simmer for 20 minutes.
2   Season well with freshly milled black pepper and a little salt. Add half the sweetcorn.
3   Liquidize in a food processor or blender.
4   Add the remaining sweetcorn, the milk and thyme and return to the heat. Bring up to the boil and adjust the seasoning before serving.

For two portions, simply halve the ingredients. For a more substantial meal, add grated reduced-fat Cheddar cheese and serve with a stick of celery and wholemeal or granary bread.

## Beef and Bean Goulash

SERVES 4
  2 tablespoons oil
  1 large or 2 small onions, chopped
  6 oz (175 g) carrots, diced
12 oz (350 g) stewing steak, trimmed and diced
  4 teaspoons paprika pepper
10 fl oz (300 ml) beef stock
  1 × 14 oz (400 g) tin tomatoes
  1½ tablespoons tomato purée
  1 teaspoon dried thyme
  1 bay leaf
    Black pepper and salt
  1 × 15 oz (425 g) tin red kidney beans
  3 tablespoons natural yogurt

1   Heat the oil in a deep-sided frying pan or heavy-bottomed saucepan and fry the onions and carrots for 10 minutes. Push these to one side and briskly brown the meat on all sides.
2   Stir in the paprika, coating the meat, and then add all the remaining ingredients except the beans and yogurt.

3   Cover and simmer gently for 1½ hours, until the meat is tender.
Add the beans and continue cooking for 10 minutes.
4   Remove the bay leaf and adjust the seasoning. Remove from
the heat and stir in the yogurt.
5   Serve with brown rice or baked potatoes.

4 oz (125 g) of dried beans can be used instead of the
tinned ones. They should be soaked overnight and then
boiled in fresh water for about 1 hour until soft. White
and black kidney, flageolets and haricot beans all make
good alternatives to the red kidney beans

The goulash freezes well, but remove portions from
the pan for freezing before adding the yogurt.

Unrefined fibre-rich foods have been recommended
throughout the book. All the recipes using vegetables
and fruit contribute dietary fibre. Brown rice, wholewheat pasta and potatoes in their jackets are suggested
as accompaniments to many of the recipes, and these
are good sources of fibre as well. Some recipes included
in other chapters are also worthy of special mention
here because they too are rich in fibre: quick fruit
crumble (page 27), creamy pasta (page 59), quick pizza
(page 73), creamed vegetable curry (page 88), bean
salad (page 89), spaghetti with tomato lentil bolognaise
(page 80), spicy peanut dip with crudités (page 97),
vegetable and nut loaf (page 98), macaroni casserole
(page 104), date and apple tea-bread (page 105), banana
fig cake (page 115).

# 7 QUICK AND EASY MEALS

Meals cooked when time is short run the risk of being rather boring and poorly balanced. It may be tempting just to reheat a pie or buy fish and chips and neglect other vegetables. But food doesn't have to be dull or unhealthy just because there is little time for cooking. The answer lies in planning and preparing in advance, using fresh ingredients that are quickly prepared and cooked, and making the best of ready-prepared foods.

*Planning and Preparation*
- If you know you are going to be in a hurry when preparing your next meal, as well as preparing your vegetables in advance assemble the necessary utensils so that they are ready for use.
- Knowing your cooker well is essential for cooking in a hurry. Try to remember at what level your burner keeps a particular pan of food simmering without boiling over. Learn too whether your oven is quick, slow or average. Fan ovens tend to heat food more quickly and many ovens have their thermostat set too high or too low. For successful grilling it is useful to know at what height to position food under your grill and how long to leave it there, when it is set at a particular heat. This sort of knowledge considerably reduces the time needed for checking food, freeing you to prepare a salad or slice a loaf of bread.
- Many recipes can be simplified with little or no loss

of appeal. Brown vegetables with the meat for a casserole rather than cooking them separately and dirtying an extra dish. Use tomato purée to thicken a casserole (if the recipe calls for tinned tomatoes, the purée can also replace them). This saves making flour and water roux and avoids the need for careful stirring.

- Generally, one-pot meals are quick and save on washing up.
- The freezer and the microwave oven are, of course, invaluable aids to the cook in a hurry (see pages 34, 35).
- In the chapter entitled 'Cooking for One or Two' (page 30), ideas are provided to prevent a disproportionate amount of time being spent in cooking for small numbers. It is not always possible to find the time to plan and prepare ahead. This is where the choice of ingredients is so important.

*Convenient Foods*
The following fresh foods are quickly cooked and prepared, and are far healthier than many pre-prepared foods, so they make an ideal basis for a meal in a hurry: poultry livers, lamb's kidneys, chops, fish fillets, eggs, cheese, avocados, cucumber, beansprouts, chicory, watercress, Chinese leaf, tomatoes, fresh fruit. As well as using these ingredients, you will also find many pre-prepared foods extremely helpful.

*Making the Most of Pre-prepared Foods*
Manufactured foods tend to be high in fat, sugar and salt. Therefore, when relying on pre-prepared foods, choose accompaniments that are low in these dietary components. Also avoid adding any extra salt, sugar or fat to the meal. For example, when using ham or bacon

in a dish, avoid adding a stock cube or salt. A bought wholemeal quiche will be high in fat and probably in salt. This can be balanced by serving it with a plain green salad (or one tossed with lemon juice) and some tasty crusty bread, which doesn't require butter.

The following foods are suitable pre-prepared foods to stock:

Ham.
Tinned fish, e.g. tuna, pilchards.
Tinned beans – drained of salted, sweetened water.
Tinned or sieved tomatoes, tomato purée.
Frozen vegetables, e.g. peas, beans, stew pack, diced mixed vegetables.
Bread sauce mix, stuffing mix, dried breadcrumbs.
Tinned fruit in natural juice.
Crunchy cereal, digestive biscuits.
Long-life milk and cream.
Long-life fruit juice or fruit juice concentrate, such as apple.
Boil-in-the-bag frozen fish.
Wholemeal quiche.
Frozen wholemeal pastry.
Bought wholemeal scones.

## Quick Meals

*Snacks*

TOMATO STUFFED WITH COTTAGE CHEESE

Scoop the centre out of a large tomato and mix with flavoured cottage cheese or the plain variety, to which you have added a teaspoon of pickle. Stuff the tomato with the mixture.

PITTA BREAD PIZZA

See the recipe on page 73.

CHEESE ON TOAST

Place sliced tomato and herbs on wholemeal toast, plus finely sliced onion, celery or green pepper if desired. Cover with reduced-fat Cheddar cheese and grill until lightly browned.

FISH ON TOAST

Mash tinned pilchards in tomato sauce with a pinch of thyme and finely chopped green pepper and celery. Spread on wholemeal toast, sprinkle with Parmesan cheese and grill.

STUFFED BAKED POTATO

Slice open a baked potato and fill it with one of the following: grated cheese and tinned sweetcorn; tinned ratatouille with grated cheese or chopped nuts; flavoured cottage cheese or baked beans heated with a little curry powder.

MAIN MEAL SOUP

Add frozen or left-over vegetables to tinned or packet soup. When ready to serve, either add grated cheese or beat in an egg. Accompany with a wholemeal roll.

CURRIED BEANS

Simmer half a finely sliced onion (with diced green pepper and celery if available) in 3–4 tablespoons water, until soft. Stir in 2–3 teaspoons curry powder and a tin of baked beans. Serve with pitta bread, rice or toast when the beans are heated through.

OPEN SANDWICHES

As a base use dark rye bread, a muffin sliced in half, a

warmed potato cake or halved crusty white or brown stick. Cover it with cooked meat or fish, cheese or egg and salad vegetables. For example, place crisp lettuce on a slice of dark rye bread, add a rollmop herring (unrolled), top with a dessertspoon of natural yogurt or fromage frais and finish with a slice of tomato, cucumber and/or green pepper.

STUFFED PITTA BREAD

See the recipe on page 98.

STUFFED AVOCADO

See the recipe on page 37.

SCRAMBLED EGG WITH SWEETCORN

Add drained tinned sweetcorn to the beaten egg mixture. When cooked, serve with toast or bread rolls and a tomato or green salad.


## Main Meals

CHICKEN LIVER AND VEGETABLE CASSEROLE

See the recipe on page 75.

CHICKEN LIVERS WITH SHERRY

Lightly fry an onion and 8 oz (250 g) chicken livers in a little oil. Add a 7 oz (200 g) tin of tomatoes and half a stock cube, a dessertspoon of dried sage and a tablespoon of sherry. Simmer for about 15 minutes, until the liver is tender. Serve with an easily prepared vegetable or salad and rice, potatoes or warmed pitta bread. Serves 2.

QUICK COBBLER

Warm half a tin of condensed celery or mushroom soup

and add 6 oz (175 g) cooked chopped chicken or lean pork. Bake in a hot oven in a greased fireproof dish for about 20 minutes with a cobbler topping. Make the topping by rubbing $\frac{3}{4}$ oz (20 g) margarine into 3 oz (75 g) self-raising wholemeal flour and then mixing with a little milk to make a soft, thick dough. Cut the dough into rounds $\frac{1}{2}$ in. (1 cm) thick and brush with milk. Serves 2.

### SMOKED FISH WITH VEGETABLES

Place a smoked fish fillet over 3–4 oz (75–125 g) frozen mixed vegetables in an ovenproof dish with a lid. Add 4 tablespoons tomato juice and a pinch of mixed herbs and bake for about 30 minutes in a medium oven.

### CREAMY PASTA

See the recipe on page 72.

## *Desserts*

### LEMON SYLLABUB

See the recipe on page 61.

### FRUIT YOGURT WITH CRUNCHY TOPPING

Mix 3–4 oz (75–125 g) fresh or tinned fruit in natural juice with half a small carton of natural yogurt. Top with half a crumbled digestive biscuit or 1 tablespoon of crunchy cereal.

### BLACKCURRANT MUESLI

Soak overnight in the fridge: 4 oz (125 g) muesli, a small carton of natural yogurt, about 8 tablespoons low-fat milk and a small tin of blackcurrants in natural juice. Sweeten to taste. Serves 3.

PEACH CREAM

Slice a small peach and marinate it in a dessertspoon of brandy, if available. Mix with a small carton of set natural yogurt and about 1 teaspoon clear honey. Chill before serving with a biscuit.

QUICK FRUIT SALAD

Mix a small tin of fruit in natural juice with a few frozen strawberries or raspberries and a sliced banana. Top with a few chopped nuts or sunflower seeds. Serves 2–3.

FRUIT CREAM SCONE

Slice open a scone and cover each half with a dollop of fromage frais. Top with a piece of tinned or fresh peach, apricot or pineapple – or a strawberry, raspberry or loganberry.

CREAM LOG

This is a rich dessert for special occasions and should accompany a main course low in fat. Dip the contents of a packet of chocolate chip or nut chip biscuits into sherry. Beat a 7 oz (200 g) carton of whipping cream until stiff and use some of it to sandwich all the biscuits together to form a log shape. Cover the log with the remaining cream and refrigerate for about 6 hours or overnight. To serve, cut diagonally in thin slices. Serves 4–6.

## Recipes

### Quick Pizza
SERVES 1
  1 slice of wholemeal pitta bread
  4 tablespoons sieved or chopped tomatoes (see page 74)

½ small onion, finely chopped
  Good pinch of mixed herbs, marjoram or oregano
1½ oz (40 g) low-fat Cheddar cheese, grated
  Black pepper

*Optional extras*
2–3 mushrooms, thinly sliced
3–4 thin slices red or green pepper
1 oz (25 g) garlic sausage, ham or salami, sliced
3 anchovies
  A few olives

1   Pre-heat the oven to 325°F/170°C/gas mark 3.
2   Cover the bread with the tomatoes, then add the onion and sprinkle on the herbs.
3   Add any extra ingredients and top with grated cheese.
4   Cook in the oven on a baking sheet for about 20 minutes, until the cheese is beginning to brown.
5   Add freshly ground black pepper and serve with a crisp salad.

To avoid opening a jar, packet or tin of tomatoes, use instead 1 heaped tablespoon tomato purée mixed with 3 tablespoons water.

For other ideas with pitta bread see pages 33 and 98.

*Fish Pie*
SERVES 3
1¼ lb (625 g) potatoes
  6 tablespoons plus 9 fl oz (275 ml) semi-skimmed milk
  Black pepper
10 fl oz (300 ml) packet parsley sauce mix
10 oz (300 g) thin fillet of cod, coley, haddock or plaice
  1 small onion, chopped
¼ green pepper, cut into strips
  1 tablespoon breadcrumbs

1   Pre-heat the oven to 400°F/200°C/gas mark 6.
2   Roughly chop the potatoes and boil in water, or cook in the microwave until soft (follow the instruction booklet for your

particular model). Add the 6 tablespoons of milk and black pepper and mash well. (Do not add salt as the sauce is salty.)

3  Make the sauce using the 9 fl oz (275 ml) milk.

4  If the fish is thick, slice it into thinner fillets. Cut into strips roughly 3 in. (7.5 cm) long and 1 in. (2.5 cm) wide.

5  Roll up the fish with a little onion and green pepper and place at the bottom of a medium-sized ovenproof dish.

6  Cover the fish with the sauce and top with the mashed potato. Sprinkle the breadcrumbs on top and 'fluff up' with a fork.

7  Set on a baking sheet and bake in the oven for 30 minutes. Serve with a green vegetable, cauliflower or carrots.

To serve two, simply reduce the quantity of fish to 7–8 oz (200–250 g) and the amount of potato to 12 oz (350 g). The dish is delicious made with smoked fish, but this requires a home-made white sauce without added salt.

## *Chicken Liver and Vegetable Hot Pot*

SERVES 2

1 dessertspoon oil
1 rasher bacon, diced
8 oz (250 g) chicken livers
6 oz (175 g) frozen stewpack vegetables
4 tablespoons orange juice
$\frac{1}{2}$ teaspoon marjoram
  Pepper and salt

1  Heat the oil and fry the bacon and livers until brown on all sides, 5–10 minutes.

2  Add the vegetables, orange juice and marjoram and season with pepper. Simmer for 15 minutes. Add a little salt if required.

3  Serve with boiled brown rice and, if there is sufficient time, green beans.

# 8 GOOD-VALUE MEALS

Food may become a more major item of expenditure in retirement as the proportion of income spent on food increases. Getting good value for money from meals can therefore be very important. Economies can be made through good planning and avoiding waste of both food and fuel. This can leave a little spare cash for a few exciting extras. Those few treats can make all the difference between boredom and great pleasure from your food.

Ideas for getting value for money when shopping are included in chapter 1 'Basic Nutrition Know-how' (page 3).

## Planning Ahead

- Plan meals around the following foods which represent excellent value for money. Although they may sound rather mundane foods, with a little imagination they can all be turned into exciting dishes. For example coley can be turned into a vegetable and fish curry. Oats can be used in a mouthwatering fruit crumble (see page 27), or in the base for a cheesecake (see page 113). Dried beans can be included in a delicious bean salad (see page 89), or used in a tasty casserole (see page 65).

  Wholemeal bread – particularly large loaves.
  Porridge oats, wholemeal and white flour.
  Potatoes and most vegetables and fruit in season.

Long-life fruit juice, frozen peas and beans in 2 lb (1 kg) or large packs.
Oily fish, e.g. mackerel, herring, sardines, pilchards, tuna.
Coley.
Liver, kidney, bacon hock joint.
Dried beans and lentils.
Milk, eggs.
Off-cuts of cheese for cooking.
Margarine, corn and soya oil.

- A store cupboard of extra items like sherry and brandy for cooking, cider or wine vinegar, spices and flavourings can be built up by buying one item each week or two. This prevents the cost being a barrier to cooking something new, simply because two or three extra items are needed all at once.
- Planning different meals based on the same main ingredient allows larger, more economical packs to be bought (see 'Variety from the Same Ingredients', page 33). Every effort should be made to vary the texture, colour and type of meal to prevent boredom. Also buying different foods from week to week helps to ensure that your diet is sufficiently varied and adequate nutritionally.
- Plan meals for a few days ahead, carefully thinking how any left-overs can be put to good use. Will there, for example, be a little celery or half an onion left over that can be used in a nourishing lentil soup?

## Cooking Economically

- It is so easy to over-produce when cooking for just one or two. But be strict about reducing the quantities in recipes. Throwing out surplus from expen-

sive meat, fish or cheese is so wasteful. However, eating more than you need will do no good to your waistline either, so only cook surplus when you have clear plans for the extra at another meal.

● It is surprising how little meat or fish you require when cooking for one or two. As a guide the following portion sizes are suitable for one helping:

4 oz (125 g) raw beef, lamb, pork, chicken (off the bone).
3 oz (75 g) cooked meat or fish.
3–5 oz (75–150 g) wet fish.
1–2 eggs.
1½ oz (40 g) cheese.
2–3 oz (50–75 g) dried beans or lentils (dry weight).
3–4 oz (75–125 g) vegetables (more of potatoes).

Where recipes include meat and cheese or meat and beans, you need less of both.

- Many recipes can be made more economical by substituting cheaper ingredients for expensive ones. This can be particularly useful in the case of vegetables or fruit which are expensive when out of season. For example, tinned tomatoes can replace fresh ones; celery can be used instead of fennel; or chicken breast, lean pork, rabbit, or chicken livers may take the place of a prime steak or veal.

*Economy with Fuel*
- Water that is just boiling is the same temperature as vigorously boiling water. So do not pay to fill the room with steam! Use well-fitting lids and steam vegetables over other boiling foods. Also cook different vegetables in the same pan.
- Use the minimum amount of water in the kettle and keep it free of scale.
- There is no need to pre-heat the oven for many single dishes like stews, casseroles, milk puddings, garlic bread, baked vegetables and fruits. Use the oven for several items at a time.
- Turn off an electric oven or grill a little before the end of cooking. Similarly, an egg can be soft-boiled by bringing it to the boil and then leaving it to sit in the hot water for about six minutes, with the heat turned off.
- One-pot meals save on fuel as well as washing up.
- Use the smallest pan you can, making sure it completely covers the burner. Use only the minimum of water.
- Make use of the specialized cooking appliances you have such as a toaster, electric kettle, slow-cooker, infra-red grill or microwave. These are efficient in heating the food more directly. For example, boil water in the kettle and transfer to the saucepan when cooking spaghetti or potatoes.

# Recipes

## *Liver with Orange and Thyme*

SERVES 2

1 dessertspoon oil
1 oz (25 g) bacon, diced
1 medium onion, chopped
8 oz (250 g) pig's liver, sliced
6 tablespoons beef stock (made from $\frac{1}{3}$ stock cube)
  Grated rind of $\frac{1}{2}$ orange
$\frac{1}{2}$ teaspoon thyme
3 tablespoons orange juice
2 tablespoons natural yogurt

1   Heat the oil and fry the bacon and onion for 5 minutes. Add the liver and briskly brown on all sides.
2   Add the stock, orange rind and thyme and simmer for 30 minutes, until tender.
3   Add the orange juice and continue cooking for 2–3 minutes. Take off the heat and stir in the yogurt.
4   Serve with wholewheat pasta, noodles or potatoes and lightly cooked cabbage or spring greens.

## *Spaghetti with Tomato Lentil Bolognaise*

SERVES 4

1 tablespoon oil
2 cloves garlic, finely chopped
1 medium onion, finely chopped
1 × 14 oz (400 g) tin tomatoes
8 oz (250 g) red lentils, washed
16 fl oz (475 ml) water
$1\frac{1}{2}$ teaspoons basil or marjoram
Black pepper and salt
2 oz (50 g) wholewheat spaghetti per serving
1 tablespoon natural yogurt per serving

1   Heat the oil and fry the garlic and onion for 5 minutes in a heavy-bottomed or non-stick pan.
2   Add the tomatoes, lentils and water and simmer for about 35 minutes, until the lentils are soft. Add more water to prevent boiling dry if necessary.

3  Add the herbs and pepper and salt to taste. Stir well and continue cooking for 2 minutes.
4  Meanwhile, boil the spaghetti for 20 minutes, until just cooked.
5  Spoon the sauce over the spaghetti, top with 1 tablespoon yogurt and a little freshly ground pepper. Serve with a green salad.

The sauce freezes well, so half can be stored for another occasion.

# 9 MORE FUN WITH VEGETABLES

One of the marvellous things about vegetables is the fact that they are packed with vitamins and minerals and they are filling without being fattening. It is, therefore, well worthwhile planning meals around them, even though they may seem an unnecessary effort to prepare for just one or two people. In particular they are a key source of vitamins A, C, folic acid and other B vitamins. They are also valuable for fibre, iron, calcium and other minerals. It is because of these nutritional qualities that vegetables help you to radiate good health through your skin, hair, eyes and figure.

It is wise to include vegetables in two meals each day, even if it is only a sliced tomato or stick of celery with a sandwich for one of the meals.

## Getting the Most from Vegetables

To make the best of the nutritional value and taste of vegetables there are a few basic rules.

- Eat vegetables as fresh as possible as they lose vitamins, flavour and texture on storage. Clean and cut them as close to the meal time as possible. Avoid soaking for long periods, otherwise valuable nutrients leach away.
- Serve vegetables raw as often as possible. This way you obtain the maximum vitamins. If chewing or

indigestion are a problem, shred or finely slice the vegetables.

- When cooking vegetables, use the minimum water and cook only lightly. Steaming, stir-frying (using just a little oil), baking and cooking in a microwave with only minimal water are all good cooking methods to choose.
- Try to eat vegetables as soon as they are cooked; avoid using a hot-plate to keep vegetables warm, other than occasionally to ease the anxiety of entertaining.
- Never add bicarbonate of soda when cooking vegetables even though this enhances their colour as this destroys vitamin C and some B vitamins.
- Whenever possible, use the vegetable cooking water as a stock for soups, casseroles and sauces.
- Use a wide variety of vegetables as they differ in the vitamins and minerals they contribute to the diet.
- Salad vegetables should be stored, loosely wrapped, in the bottom of the fridge and other vegetables such as potatoes and carrots should be stored in a cool dry place. If they are kept in a plastic bag, this should have holes punctured in it to allow air to circulate, otherwise the vegetables will quickly rot.

## Fresh or Frozen?

You can't beat fresh vegetables straight from your garden, or a local market garden, for flavour, texture and nutritional value. Nonetheless, when several days have elapsed between the harvesting of these and their reaching your plate, frozen vegetables can be of higher quality. Top-quality frozen vegetables are often frozen within hours of picking. Provided that the refrigeration conditions are good, they can be superior to stale 'fresh' vegetables. Frozen vegetables usually work out more expensive, except when fresh ones are in short supply due to bad weather or because they are out of season. The convenience value of frozen vegetables, particularly when catering for small numbers, is another important consideration. Unlike many pre-prepared foods, frozen vegetables offer good nutritional value.

Tinned or dried vegetables (excluding pulses) are of inferior quality, having lost vitamins, minerals, flavour, texture and colour during processing. They are useful if used just occasionally to save time, money or effort.

## The Enormous Scope of Vegetables

Explore the full potential of vegetables. They can be so much more than just a boiled accompaniment to a main meal. Stuff them with meat, fish, nuts or cheese, rice and herb mixtures. Use them as snacks, appetizers, garnishes and sandwich fillings or for their colour, texture and taste in casseroles or meat or nut loaves.

If you are in a rut with your cooking or need something different for a special occasion, vegetables will probably offer the solution. An interesting selection of vegetables, chosen from the wide variety available, can provide a special touch to meals, without incurring the expense of fillet steak or lobster and without the calories of cream and exotic cheeses.

### Stretching a Meal
Stew and casserole recipes can be adapted to include extra vegetables, while the meat quantity is reduced. This saves money, apart from increasing the fibre and reducing the fat content of the meal.

*Colours*
It is a good habit to think of the overall colour of meals. You may, for example, like to select a variety of vegetables, all of different shades of green or red. Otherwise a selection of vegetables ranging from white, yellow, green and brown to red, served at one meal, can have mouth-watering appeal. Simply mixing vegetables such as peas, celery and carrots can add interest to an everyday meal

*Exotic Vegetables*
It can be fun to experiment with some of the more exotic vegetables from time to time such as artichokes, aubergines, bean sprouts, celeriac, okra, pumpkin, salsify or yams. Roast, steam, boil or bake them as appropriate, or use them in salads (see the suggestions below). Some of the larger supermarkets produce information sheets and leaflets providing ideas on how to prepare and serve some of the more unusual but flavoursome vegetables and fruit. It is well worth looking out for these.

*Soups*
Nearly all vegetables make delightful soups. For people who find that some vegetables are difficult to chew, or cause indigestion or flatulence, soup can be a marvellous way of eating them. Rather than thicken this type of soup with flour, which spoils the flavour, liquidize or blend the vegetables. If you're not keen on a smooth texture, retain a few vegetable pieces. Natural yogurt swirled on to the top of the soup just before serving gives added attraction and taste. For a main course, look for recipes using lentils, dried beans or split peas. Alternatively, serve with grated cheese.

## Salads

It is so easy to think of salads as just lettuce, cucumber and tomato. In fact, most vegetables can be used in salads, although a few need cooking first – but usually only lightly. Experiment with some of the following in salads:

Asparagus – boiled or steamed.

Avocado – sliced lengthways and widthways into wedge-shaped pieces, tossed with lemon juice and used in a mixed salad.

Beansprouts – use raw; try tossed with orange or lemon juice.

Dried beans – cooked (see the recipe for bean salad on page 89).

Runner beans – lightly boiled.

Cabbage, red or white – shredded.

Carrots – grated or shredded.

Celeriac – grated coarsely and tossed in a citrus juice or vinegar.

Celery or fennel – finely sliced.

Chicory – whole leaves.

Chinese leaf, Webbs or Cos lettuce – use whole leaves or shred coarsely.

Courgettes or marrow – blanched.

Endive or Iceberg lettuce – chopped into manageable pieces.

Dried or fresh fruit, or fruit tinned in natural juice.

Peas – lightly cooked.

Peppers – in rings, diced or in strips.

Radicchio or other red lettuce – in a mixed green salad with vinaigrette dressing or used as a garnish.

Radish, red – sliced, or whole with $\frac{1}{2}$ in. (1 cm) of stem.

Radish, white – grated or sliced.

Salsify – cooked for 10–15 minutes and then tossed in lemon juice or vinegar.

Spring onions – whole (including a little stem) or sliced.

Brussel sprouts – grated raw.
Sweetcorn – cooked.
Watercress – eat very fresh.

*Herbs*
Freshly chopped herbs are also delicious in salads. A plain green salad of crisp lettuce can be turned into something special by adding a variety of fresh herbs. Try some of the following: basil, borage, chives, coriander, fennel leaves, hyssop, lovage, marjoram, mint (various kinds), parsley and tarragon. Toss with salad dressing made from equal quantities of oil and cider or wine vinegar.

## Vegetarianism

A vegetarian diet excludes only meat and fish. Vegans, on the other hand, avoid all animal produce, including eggs, milk and cheese. There are many misunderstandings about vegetarianism. Most of us remember being told to 'eat up our meat to become strong and healthy'. Yet you may be surprised to learn that vegetarians are generally healthier, with reduced rates of obesity, coronary heart disease, hypertension, disorders of the large bowel, some cancers and gall stones. In addition the level of cholesterol in the blood tends to be lower in vegetarians. It is therefore not surprising that there is a growing interest in vegetarianism. However, it is easy to be discouraged by difficulties when eating out and a lack of knowledge of vegetarian recipes. It is true that to enjoy vegetarian food a little more effort is required in preparing meals than when simply grilling a chop.

Recently a popular new demi-vegetarian way of eating evolved, which helped to dispel the misguided view that vegetarians are cranks who eat boring diets.

This way of eating enables you to enjoy the best of both worlds. A number of red meat meals are replaced by tasty vegetarian dishes. Chicken and fish are still eaten, as is an occasional steak if desired.

If you eat a meal in a vegetarian restaurant or at the home of a vegetarian, you may be amazed by the new world of exciting and flavoursome food. For those new to vegetarian cooking, cheese and nut dishes can be the most appealing. Good examples are a nut roast (see page 98), a vegetable and nut curry (see page 88) or a vegetarian lasagne.

Changing to vegetarianism with inadequate knowledge can lead to an unhealthy diet. It is essential that plenty of non-meat sources of iron are eaten (see page 5). Also meat and fish need to be replaced with other good protein sources such as nuts, seeds and pulses. Simply substituting meat and fish with cheese and eggs can result in a diet high in saturated fats. It is therefore important that the pulses and nuts are used. As a general guide the following are suitable portion sizes for a main meal:

2–3 oz (50–75 g) dried beans or lentils (dried weight)
1½–2 oz (40–50 g) nuts or seeds.

## Recipes

### Creamed Vegetable Curry
SERVES 2
  1 tablespoon oil
  2 cloves garlic, crushed
  1 medium onion, chopped
  2 teaspoons ground coriander
  1 teaspoon ground cumin
  ¼ teaspoon turmeric
  ¼ teaspoon chilli powder

1 tablespoon fresh root ginger, finely chopped
1 × 7 oz (200 g) tin tomatoes, chopped
1 lb (500 g) chopped mixed vegetables, e.g. cauliflower florets, green beans, spinach, carrot, celery, pepper, courgettes
5 tablespoons hot water
$\frac{1}{4}$ teaspoon salt
$1\frac{1}{2}$ (40 g) chunk of creamed coconut, cut into pieces
2 oz (50 g) nuts, e.g. cashews

1   Heat the oil in a deep non-stick frying pan with a lid or a heavy-bottomed saucepan, and fry the garlic and onion gently for about 7 minutes.
2   Add the spices and the ginger and cook for a further 2 minutes.
3   Add the tomatoes, vegetables, water and salt. Cover and simmer for about 25 minutes, until the vegetables are cooked.
4   Add the pieces of creamed coconut and stir until dissolved and thoroughly heated through.
5   Serve the curry on a bed of brown rice topped with nuts.

## Bean Salad

SERVES ABOUT 6
5 oz (150 g) frozen green beans
1 × 15 oz (425 g) tin red kidney beans, drained and rinsed
1 × 15 oz (425 g) tin borlotti, haricot or butter beans, drained and rinsed
$\frac{1}{2}$ × 11 oz (325 g) tin sweetcorn, drained
3 tablespoons chopped fresh herbs, e.g. tarragon, chives, parsley, thyme, basil, marjoram *or* 2 teaspoons dried mixed herbs

*For the dressing*:
1 teaspoon mustard powder
$1\frac{1}{2}$ tablespoons wine or cider vinegar
$1\frac{1}{2}$ tablespoons olive oil
2 cloves garlic, crushed
Black pepper and salt

1   Boil the green beans for 5 minutes, until cooked. Drain.
2   Add to the tinned beans and sweetcorn and stir in the herbs.
3   Prepare the dressing by blending the mustard with $\frac{1}{2}$ tablespoon vinegar. Then add the remaining vinegar, oil, garlic and seasoning.

4   Pour the dressing over the beans and combine well.

This stores well in the fridge in a covered plastic or glass container and can be used over three days. Instead of using ready-cooked beans, 3 oz (75 g) dried beans can replace each tin of beans. These need to be soaked overnight and boiled till soft in fresh water.

## Coleslaw
SERVES 4
8 oz (250 g) white cabbage
4 oz (125 g) carrots
2 tablespoons raisins *or* sultanas

*For the dressing:*
1 teaspoon mustard powder
1 tablespoon vinegar
3 tablespoons natural yogurt
$\frac{1}{2}$ tablespoon oil
2 tablespoons low-calorie salad cream

1   Shred the cabbage and carrots – in a food processor if available.
2   Make the dressing by mixing the mustard with the vinegar and then stirring in the yogurt, oil and salad cream.
3   Add the dressing and dried fruit to the vegetables and toss well.
4   Chill before serving.

This will keep in the fridge for up to three days.

# 10 EATING OUT WELL

With time to go on outings, eating meals away from home can be an important aspect of retirement. Also, if for many years you have relied on a meal in a restaurant at work or the odd meal 'on expenses', then a break from three meals a day at home may be very welcome.

Pubs and sandwich bars can provide meals that are reasonable value for money. However, it may be difficult to find something that suits your needs when eating out. By retirement age many people have developed special dietary needs such as for diabetes, a fat intolerance, or a tendency to indigestion brought on by certain foods. A low-fat diet may be needed for heart disease or for weight control.

One of the joys of eating out can be the escape from planning a meal. However, simply prepared picnics can provide far more freedom. You can eat what you need at the time and place of your choice. There are, also of course, the financial considerations. Eating out can seem expensive for those accustomed to a subsidized canteen or an expense account. A picnic can make an outing far more economical.

Suggestions are provided below for simply prepared and interesting picnics. For those preferring to buy a meal out there is advice on what to look out for.

## Picnics

*Savouries*

- Wholemeal cheese scones.
- Tandoori chicken drumsticks (see the recipe on page 27).
- Stuffed pitta bread (see the recipe on page 98).
- Home-made pizza on a bap or muffin base, or a bought one lightly cooked.
- Pasta salad: cooked pasta (or rice) mixed with cooked chicken, ham, tuna fish, nuts or cooked beans plus sweetcorn, diced pepper, sliced celery or green beans, diced apple or pineapple – and a dressing. Use a vinaigrette dressing made from half-oil and half-vinegar, or the dressing used for coleslaw (see the recipe on page 90).
- A slice of vegetable and nut loaf (see the recipe on page 98).
- A slice of meat loaf (see the recipe on page 39).
- A slice of savoury wholemeal flan – bought or home-made.
- A stuffed fresh tomato (see the recipe on page 69).
- A pot of flavoured cottage cheese with interesting cheese biscuits or bread.

*Vegetables*

- Crudités with peanut dip (see the recipe on page 97) or blue cheese dip (see page 110).
- Tomatoes.
- Sticks of celery or pieces of fennel.
- Radishes.
- Chicory or Chinese leaves.
- Cucumber – slice during the picnic.
- Bean salad (see the recipe on page 89).

- Coleslaw (see the recipe on page 90).
- Potato salad – cubes of cooked potato mixed with equal quantities of natural yogurt and low-calorie salad cream, plus a pinch of curry powder and black pepper.

*Sandwiches*

With a little thought and imagination, sandwiches can make an exciting and nutritious meal. Vary the bread used both in type and shape. But remember that, nutritionally, wholegrain varieties are the best. Experiment with some of the following breads: baps, wholemeal or flavoured muffins, bread rolls, pitta bread, bread with sesame seeds, soda bread, French stick, Vienna loaf, rye and mixed-grain breads, and varieties with poppy or caraway seeds.

Here are some suggestions for sandwich fillings:

- Grated cheese and diced celery or fennel with lettuce.
- Cooked chicken and diced apple, mixed with a little natural yogurt and low-calorie mayonnaise or salad cream.
- Bread moistened with French dressing instead of margarine, lined with salad in season and filled with tinned tuna, salmon, tongue or ham.
- Mashed hard-boiled egg mixed with a teaspoon of low-calorie salad cream and a quarter of a slice of ham diced, some cress and black pepper.
- Sliced banana and finely chopped nuts; the sandwich should be covered with cling-film to prevent discolouration.
- Hard-boiled egg mashed with a pinch of curry powder, a little natural yogurt and low-calorie salad cream, and mixed with diced green pepper.

- Meat loaf (see the recipe on page 39), French mustard, sliced tomatoes and crisp lettuce.
- Avocado mashed with curd cheese or fromage frais and a little mango chutney; lettuce to line the bread. The sandwich should be covered with cling-film to prevent discolouration.

Diced pineapple and sliced peach are also useful ingredients when making interesting sandwiches.

*Desserts*
- Fruit salad or fruit trifle in a carton.
- A carton of fruit yogurt.
- Fresh fruit in season.
- Mixed dried fruit.
- Flapjack.
- Wholemeal scone.
- Scotch pancake.
- Two slices of malt loaf sandwiched together with thinly spread margarine.
- A slice of tea-bread (see the recipe on page 105).
- A slice of banana fig cake (see the recipe on page 115).

## What to Look for When Eating Out

It can be difficult to eat healthily when eating out. This is partly because of a lack of suitable menu choices. Also, it's difficult to know what the various dishes contain. Meals in a restaurant are not labelled, with a list of ingredients in descending order of quantity used, like foods in a supermarket!

It is really a matter of balance when eating out. If you fancy a lasagne, which will probably be high in fat, why not compensate for this by eating a crusty roll without

butter and a fresh salad without an oil or mayonnaise dressing, and having fruit for dessert? If eating out is a rare occasion for you, it does not really matter about indulging in dishes high in fat, sugar and salt – provided that they don't upset your digestion.

On the whole, it is wise to make the most sensible choice available, but obviously of something you enjoy. It is best to exercise your willpower over the accompaniments as you are likely to have the most control over these. There is usually scope for avoiding the addition of lots of cream, butter, dressings and sauces, as well as individual choice over drinks.

For those who like a dessert other than fruit, the following are less fattening than many other desserts: a soufflé, ice cream, sorbet, crème caramel or a choux pastry item like an éclair.

Sometimes healthier alternatives can be provided if you enquire. For example, it can be worth asking for skimmed milk, a polyunsaturated margarine, artificial sweetener, decaffeinated coffee, wholemeal bread instead of white, or a made-to-order sandwich with only thinly spread margarine.

Wholefood or vegetarian restaurants can make an excellent change even for those who normally prefer traditional English cooking. Food is usually filling and rich in fibre, vitamins and minerals. However, it is quite unlikely that some of the food will still be high in fat or sugar (probably from honey or brown sugar).

To eat well when eating out, look out for some of the following foods and dishes:

*Traditional Restaurants*
- Bread and baked or boiled potatoes – but limit the butter added.
- Plain boiled rice and pasta.
- Vegetables without butter or a sauce.
- Salads without a dressing, or just with vinegar.
- Small grilled steak.
- Lean roast meat, small to moderate portion.
- Baked or grilled fish.
- Fresh fruit, fresh fruit salad or fruit compote.

*Foreign Cooking*
- Tandoori dishes – without sauce.
- Plain boiled rice.
- Chappati.
- Shish kebab.
- Tzatziki (yogurt and cucumber dish) with pitta bread.
- Hummus (chick peas and sesame seeds) with pitta bread.
- Chinese dishes, cooked to order (avoiding foods in batter) – even so they may be high in fat and probably in salt.
- Pizza, but avoiding ones with salami, cooked sausage or extra cheese.
- Japanese cooking is particularly healthy, apart from the generous use of salt.

*Pubs and Snack Meals*
- Ploughman's snack – leave the butter and some cheese if portions of these are over-generous. Request wholemeal bread.
- Smoked mackerel salad with wholemeal bread.
- Stuffed baked potato – ask for butter not to be added if you are watching the fat.
- Sandwiches – ask for wholemeal bread and avoid salami and fillings rich in mayonnaise.
- Poached eggs.
- Baked beans.
- Wholemeal scones or tea-breads.
- Fruit yogurt.

## Recipes

*Spicy Peanut Dip with Crudités*

SERVES 4–6
*For the dip:*
1 × 5 oz (150 g) carton natural yogurt, preferably thick set, *or* fromage frais
1 rounded tablespoon crunchy or smooth peanut butter
1½ oz (40 g) medium-fat hard cheese, finely grated
1 tablespoon finely chopped green pepper, radish or celery
2–3 teaspoons lemon juice
1 clove garlic, crushed
1½ teaspoon mild curry powder

*For the crudités:*

| | |
|---|---|
| Sticks of carrot, celery, pepper, cucumber, courgette | Total weight about 8 oz (250 g) |
| Cauliflower florets | |
| Button mushrooms | |

1   Blend all the ingredients well together for the dip. Add only 2 teaspoons lemon juice if not using thick set yogurt. Chill.
2   Serve the dip in an attractive bowl in the centre of a plate and surround it with the colourful vegetables.

97

If preparing the dip for young children, use smooth peanut butter.

The crudités can be prepared in advance and stored in a plastic bag in the fridge.

### Stuffed Pitta

MAKES 6

1 × 7 oz (200 g) tin tuna fish, drained
8 oz (250 g) low-fat fromage frais
2 teaspoons lemon juice
1 rounded dessertspoon curried fruit chutney
3 slices wholemeal pitta bread

1   Flake the fish, then mix with the fromage frais.
2   Stir in the lemon juice and chutney.
3   Cut the pitta breads in half and stuff each half with the mixture.
4   Pack them firmly in a plastic box with a lid – mixture upwards.

Thick set natural yogurt can replace the fromage frais.

This dish makes an ideal starter with each stuffed half pitta bread served on a bed of crisp lettuce and garnished with tomato or red pepper.

If only part of the mixture is required for stuffing the pitta bread, the remainder can be stored, covered, in the fridge for up to two days. As an alternative, serve with salad or use to stuff a baked potato.

### Vegetable and Nut Loaf

SERVES 4

1 tablespoon oil
1 medium onion, finely chopped
2 sticks celery, finely sliced
8 oz (250 g) mushrooms, sliced
1 × 7 oz (200 g) tin tomatoes
6 oz (175 g) mixed nuts, e.g. hazelnuts and unsalted peanuts, very finely chopped
6 oz (175 g) fresh wholemeal breadcrumbs
1½ teaspoons dried mixed herbs

1 large or 2 small eggs, beaten
Black pepper and salt.

1   Pre-heat the oven to 375°F/190°C/gas mark 5.
2   Heat the oil and fry the onion and celery for 5 minutes.
3   Add the mushrooms and fry for a further 5 minutes, then add the tomatoes and simmer for 5 minutes.
4   Remove from the heat and add the remaining ingredients, mixing thoroughly.
5   Transfer to a well-greased 2 lb (1 kg) loaf tin (use non-stick if available) and bake in the oven for 40 minutes.

As an alternative, replace the mushrooms with 8 oz (250 g) sliced and chopped aubergine. For a picnic, the loaf is more manageable when cooked with two eggs. It freezes well.

# 11 FEEDING THE GRANDCHILDREN

Although it can be great fun catering for grandchildren, there is always the worry of 'Will they eat it?' and 'Will their parents approve?'. It therefore seems appropriate to provide some guidelines on current attitudes to healthy eating for children, and tips on making food appeal to the younger generation.

## A Healthy Start

- Weaning is recommended from about four months. Infant cereals or liquidized vegetables are suitable first foods. Egg white is not recommended before six months. Under one year of age current advice is to avoid the addition of salt and sugar in cooking and to avoid salty foods like ham and other processed meats, commercial soups and stocks.

- Tastes develop in childhood, so if you have a sweet or salty tooth try to curb it, even when cooking for children above a year old. As well as avoiding the addition of salt when cooking, keep the salt pot and sugar bowl off the table when your grandchildren call. They are less likely to ask for salt or sugar if they are not in sight.

- For the sake of the teeth offer desserts and confectionery (if you feel they are necessary) only with meals. Sugar does most harm, causing tooth decay, when eaten between meals. It is far better to eat a packet of sweets all in one go with a meal than to nibble them throughout the day.

- Soft drinks can be full of sugar, taking away the appetite for more nutritious foods, as well as harming the teeth. Generally choose the sugar-free varieties. Parents have different views on fruit squashes. Some are more concerned about the sugar content, preferring the sugar-free varieties, and others select those free of artificial sweeteners, colourings and preservatives but high in sugar. It might be advisable to check with the parents as to whether they have strong views on the matter.

- It is believed that atherosclerosis (build-up of fat in the arteries) can start from childhood. It therefore makes sense to avoid an excess of fatty foods like sausage rolls, chips, and crisps.

- Children benefit from the additional nutrients provided by the unrefined fibre-rich foods. They should thus be encouraged to enjoy wholemeal bread, brown rice, wholewheat pasta, pulses, vegetables and fruit. It is also important that the bowel is trained to function well from childhood and this entails eating adequate fibre.

- Young children can find it difficult to meet their energy (calorie) requirements when their diet consists mainly of foods with a low energy density, like low-fat milks and yogurt and bulky foods. (Wholemeal bread, other cereals, beans, potatoes, other vegetables and fruit are all examples of bulky foods.) This is because young children have a high energy requirement relative to their size and stomach capacity. They may also find it difficult to digest large quantities of the high-fibre foods. It is for this reason that the current advice is to give full-fat milk to children under two years. Fully skimmed milk is not advised before five years of age. There is also concern that the use of skimmed milk could result in children meeting their energy requirements by filling up on sweets and drinks full of sugar – with all the worry of decaying teeth. However, when entertaining for just a short period a toddler who drinks cow's milk, the type of milk isn't too important. If you use semi-skimmed milk, you can always compensate for this by adding a teaspoon of vegetable oil to the child's cereal or mashed potato. Some young children find too much fibre from wholegrain foods and pulses difficult to digest; if this is the case, they should be eaten only in moderation.

- Avoid a battle between parents and grandparents about giving children sweets. Children love the interest grandparents show in their achievements as well as their time and attention. These are likely to be valued far more than gifts of sweets. Nice fruits, fresh or dried, make a healthier substitute if you must buy them a snack.

## Food for Children

- Find out the children's basic likes and dislikes, which may have changed since the previous visit. Unless you know your grandchildren are 'excellent eaters', do not spend hours preparing food for them! It is much easier to ignore food fads if you've not spent too much effort on cooking to please them.
- Build meals around their likes and take a 'no fuss' approach. Do not feel shy about offering a rejected meal a few hours later when they claim to be hungry – but keep the food covered in the fridge in the meantime. Problems develop when alternatives are offered as soon as a dish is rejected.

- Finger feeding is enjoyed particularly by younger children. Individual items that are easily distinguished are usually popular, such as pieces of quiche or pizza, sausages, chicken drumsticks, or fresh fruit. There's often a preference for several small items rather than one large piece. A whole round of cheese or fish on toast may be rejected, whereas small triangular pieces may be a great success. Little bread rolls may be more popular than slices of toast. Raw vegetable sticks can be a great success, whereas cooked vegetables are often unpopular. It is worth breaking convention and offering raw vegetable sticks or raw cauliflower florets with a hot dish if this means that the children will readily eat a balanced meal.

- Funny faces and animals can easily be constructed from simple foods, giving a meal added appeal to children. A face can be made from pieces of tomato, carrot, red and green pepper, sweetcorn or celery. These can be placed on grilled cheese or scrambled egg on a toasted bap or crumpet, or on a scoop of mashed potato. A dog can be made out of three rectangular pieces of toast covered with fish, cheese or egg. One rectangle is needed for the body. A smaller one is needed for the face and the smallest rectangle, cut diagonally, makes two ears. Slices of carrot or celery can be used for legs and a pickled gherkin cut into a fan shape makes a good tail. Sweetcorn or a piece of dried fruit are suitable for an eye. The opportunities are quite endless. Pieces of cooked meat, vegetables and pasta can be substituted for the toast and raw vegetables. There really is scope for your imagination. What about creating a hedgehog or a fish?

- Convenience foods such as burgers, fish fingers and baked beans are useful, but try to select the healthier reduced-fat or lower-sugar varieties where available. Low-fat sausages or lean burgers with a wholemeal roll and a salad garnish make an adequately balanced meal. Pizza is often a favourite with children, and you can make your own with only a little effort (see page 73).

- Fruit is usually a popular and healthy choice with children. Small fruits such as grapes, cherries, sweet plums and apricots, strawberries, satsumas and dried fruit are usually appreciated. Bananas are useful too. They are nutritious and versatile. With little effort they can be turned into a banana split with ice cream or banana custard. Another healthy and simple pudding is mashed banana with natural yogurt and a digestive biscuit crumbled on top. Other suitable desserts include fruit crumble, simple fruit salad or fruit yogurt.
- Natural fruit juice is usually popular, but to reduce the cost and adverse effects on the teeth, dilute it with at least half water. For a treat try natural fruit juice diluted with soda water or sparkling mineral water.

## Recipes

### Macaroni Casserole
SERVES 4
6 oz (175 g) wholewheat macaroni
1 large onion, chopped
1 clove garlic, finely chopped (optional)
8 oz (250 g) lean minced beef
1 × 7 oz (200 g) tin tomatoes
1 tablespoon tomato purée
5 tablespoons water
1 teaspoon dried oregano
  Black pepper and salt
1 large egg yolk

7 oz (200 g) natural yogurt
3 oz (75 g) reduced-fat Cheddar cheese, grated

1   Cook the macaroni in 3 pints (1.7 litres) boiling water for 15–20 minutes, stirring occasionally.
2   Heat the oven to 350°F/180°C/gas mark 4.
3   Fry the onion, garlic (if using) and mince together until all the meat has turned brown.
4   Stir in the tomatoes, tomato purée, 3 tablespoons of water, oregano, pepper and salt and cook for 10 minutes.
5   Mix the egg yolk with the yogurt and season with pepper.
6   Grease a deep-sided 2½ pint (1.4 litre) casserole dish. Place half the macaroni at the bottom, then sprinkle on half the cheese.
7   Cover with half the mince mixture. Then add another layer of macaroni and mince.
8   Pour the yogurt mixture over the top.
9   Bake in the oven for 30 minutes, then sprinkle the remaining cheese on top and bake for a further 10 minutes.
10   Serve with salad.

About 10 fl oz (300 ml) white sauce can replace the yogurt topping. For a vegetarian version the meat can be replaced by vegetables such as chopped aubergines, mushrooms or peppers, or by baked beans; the quantity of cheese should be doubled and the sauce increased by half.

## Date and Apple Tea-bread

MAKES 12 SLICES
4 fl oz (125 ml) boiling water
1 tea-bag
8 oz (250 g) fine wholemeal self-raising flour
1 teaspoon mixed spice
1 oz (25 g) polyunsaturated margarine
1 medium-sized cooking apple, coarsely grated
4 oz (125 g) dates, chopped
4 oz (125 g) sultanas
3 fl oz (75 ml) semi-skimmed milk
1 egg, beaten

1   Pre-heat the oven to 350°F/180°C/gas mark 4.

2   Pour boiling water over the tea-bag and leave to infuse.

3   Mix the flour and spice in a bowl and rub in the margarine.

4   Stir the grated apple into the flour with the dried fruit and then make a well in the middle.

5   Add the milk to the tea and when sufficiently cool pour the liquid into the well with the egg. Stir lightly until evenly mixed.

6   Turn into a well-greased 2 lb (1 kg) loaf tin.

7   Bake in the oven for about 50 minutes, until a skewer inserted in the centre comes out clean. Alternatively, cook in a microwave, following the instruction booklet for your particular model.

8   Allow to cool for 3–5 minutes and then turn out on to a wire rack.

It is not essential to make fresh tea specially for this recipe – left-over tea can be used if you have any.

# 12 ENTERTAINING AND MORE ADVENTUROUS COOKING

When you have more time to spend with friends and relatives, it is to be expected that entertaining should be an important part of retirement. Nonetheless, serving meals for four or six can seem very hard work if you are geared up to meals for just one or two. Some tips are therefore included here to help you enjoy entertaining at every level.

## How to Enjoy Entertaining

- When entertaining for a weekend or a few days, plan ahead as much as possible. Start by writing a menu, but be a little flexible when you see what is available in the shops at an acceptable price. If you have a freezer, prepare a few dishes beforehand. Cook enough to eat with your visitors and sufficient for a meal the day you cook the dish. The finishing touches can be done when the visitors have arrived. For example, a topping can be added to a simple marinated chicken casserole. Even if you are cooking a quickly prepared dish such as chicken livers with sherry and sage (see page 71) or the quick pizza (see page 73), the basic preparation can be done in advance. For example, ready-prepared vegetables or grated cheese can be stored in the fridge ready for use.

- When planning a menu, think about the available fridge space. It can be quite tiring juggling the extra food around in the fridge, trying to make space.
- Planning ahead also means that the cost of feeding more mouths can be spread over a few weeks!
- It is easy to over-purchase when you are not accustomed to cooking for a large number. When planning the menu, calculate the quantities, based on the recommended portions per person given on page 78. Allow extra for visitors with good appetites. Buy foods just for the planned meals and snacks, but for confidence keep something spare that you can always use a week or two later if it is not required.
- Why not experiment, particularly on dishes that don't work well with small quantities? Unless you are a very skilful cook, it is worth avoiding fiddly recipes, however. With the added pressures it is so easy for something to go wrong. It is better to concentrate on interesting colours and flavours and

more exotic vegetables and fruit. It is probably also wise to avoid recipes calling for unusual ingredients (such as certain spices and flavourings) that will be wasted if you are unlikely to use them again.

- There is no need to serve rich food with lashings of cream, butter or cheese. It is quite likely that your guests, like you, care about their waistlines. Your meals can be enjoyable without being fattening. Remember to substitute yogurt for cream, fromage frais for ordinary cream cheese, reduced-fat hard cheese for the full-fat variety and polyunsaturated oil for butter. Using a good non-stick or heavy pan allows many recipes to be prepared with far less than the usual amount of fat.

- Some meals are particularly flexible when entertaining, making it easy to relax with visitors and even fit in a walk or a game while the food is cooking. Pot roasts, casseroles and salads are good from this point of view. An electric hot-plate takes away the stress of timing a hot meal, and can be invaluable when cooking for large numbers. It is not ideal for everyday use, however, particularly in the case of vegetables which deteriorate when kept warm.

- It may be daunting returning hospitality to an experienced cook if you are only a novice like many widowers, or living on your own. But do not feel shy about entertaining – everybody has the skill to entertain in some way. Tailor the event to suit your ability, such as an invitation for tea or a drink. After all, experienced cooks still like to be invited out.

## Simple Entertaining

*Drinks*
If you do not keep a store cupboard of alcoholic drinks, the following can be bought specially for a social event:

- Lambrusco, a sparkling red Italian wine (the standard variety is rather sweet but dryer versions can be found.)
- Chilled vinho verdi – white slightly sparkling Portuguese wine.
- Spritzer – medium or dry white wine topped with sparkling mineral water.
- Amontillado – medium-dry sherry to suit most tastes.
- Try this non-alcoholic alternative. Mix two parts orange juice to one part low-calorie lemonade and one part low-calorie tonic or sparkling mineral water. Top with ice and sliced or diced fruit. For a finishing touch borage, rosemary or marigold flowers, lemon balm or a herb with a variegated leaf can be frozen in the ice cubes.
- Mulled wine: see the recipe on page 116.

*Snacks*
The following snacks are suitable to serve when inviting friends round for drinks:

- Pieces of celery, 3 in. (7.5 cm) long, stuffed with (or cucumber slices covered with) one of the following: prawn or pineapple cottage cheese; or a mixture made from 1 tablespoon cottage or curd cheese with 1 teaspoon mango or curry chutney and 1 dessertspoon finely chopped green or red pepper.
- Some vegetable sticks (crudités) with a peanut dip (see the recipe on page 97). Alternatively, dip vegetables into a blue cheese dip made from 2 oz (50 g) blue cheese (grated or crumbled) mixed with 1 tablespoon lemon juice, 3 tablespoons yogurt and 1 teaspoon castor sugar.
- Smoked tinned mussels (these are inexpensive) arranged on small triangles of dark rye bread.

- A small bowl of mixed nuts and dried fruit.
- Small slices of warmed wholemeal quiche.

*Tea*

Cakes made by the creaming method and pastry can both be difficult to make well for those who lack years of experience. It may be worth looking out for home-made cakes and biscuits at bazaars and Women's Institute stalls. Otherwise try one of the following recipes which are easy to make and will look impressive:

- Coconut flapjacks. Use the recipe for the base of the cheesecake on page 113, cutting it into bars or wedges 2–3 minutes after taking it out of the oven. Remove these from the baking tray when they are cool and store them in a tin.
- Banana fig cake (see the recipe on page 115).
- Home-made or bought scones topped with fromage frais and fruit (see page 73).

## Store Cupboard for Adventurous Cooking

Meals can become the focus of the day during retirement. It is therefore important, from time to time, to include something more exciting than usual in your everyday cooking. The following foods help to add a little more adventure to cooking.

*Non-perishable Foods*

Tinned smoked mussels.
Sesame or pumpkin seeds.
Peanut butter.
Creamed coconut.
Dried figs, apricots and bananas.
Tinned fruit in natural juice.

Sieved tomatoes in a bottle, long-life carton or tin.
Olive oil.
Sherry, brandy or rum for cooking.
Soy and tabasco sauces.
Curried chutney and mango or another suitable
    chutney to accompany curry.
Coriander, cumin, turmeric and tandoori spices.

*Perishable Foods*
Fresh lemon or lime.
Fresh root ginger.
Fresh herbs – grown in the garden or indoors.
Fromage frais.
Wholemeal pitta bread or rye bread – can be stored in
    a freezer.

As well as trying some of the more exotic vegetables,
experiment with the more unusual fruits, fish, meat
and offal. Pigeon, pheasant or venison can make an
exciting change. Some of the more exotic fruits – such
as kiwi fruit, mango, pawpaw, passion fruit, rambutan,
sharon and star fruit – may seem expensive; however,
compare the cost of buying one of these delicacies for a
treat instead of chocolate, alcoholic drinks, cigarettes
or tobacco.

## Recipes

*Pigeon Casserole*
SERVES 2
1 dessertspoon oil
2 rashers bacon, diced
1 large onion, sliced
1 stick celery, finely sliced
2 prepared pigeons
1 tablespoon redcurrant jelly *or* cranberry sauce

5 fl oz (150 ml) beef stock (made with $\frac{1}{2}$ stock cube)
1 wine glass red wine
1 teaspoon dried thyme
3 oz (75 g) mushrooms, sliced
   Black pepper

1   Pre-heat the oven to 325°F/170°C/gas mark 3.
2   Heat the oil in a flameproof casserole and gently fry the bacon, onion and celery for about 10 minutes.
3   Add the pigeons and fry on each side until brown.
4   Dissolve the redcurrant jelly in the hot stock and add to the pan with the remaining ingredients.
5   Transfer to the oven and cook for 3 hours, until the pigeons are tender.

This dish is good served with sweetcorn and a green vegetable or side salad, plus some baked potatoes which you can cook alongside the casserole in the oven for the last two hours or so of its cooking time.

## *Orange and Coconut Cheesecake*

SERVES 6–8
*For the base*:
3 oz (75 g) creamed coconut, finely chopped
2 oz (50 g) soft brown sugar
1 tablespoon syrup *or* clear honey
1 dessertspoon milk
5 oz (150 g) porridge oats
$\frac{1}{2}$ teaspoon mixed spice
   Grated rind of $\frac{1}{2}$ orange

*For the filling*:
 2 eggs, separated
 1 tablespoon brown sugar
 1 tablespoon orange juice
12 oz (350 g) low-fat fromage frais
 5 oz (150 g) orange yogurt
   Grated rind of remaining $\frac{1}{2}$ orange

*To decorate (optional)*:
6–8 teaspoons fromage frais
6–8 mandarin segments *or* 6–8 slices of kiwi fruit

1   Pre-heat the oven to 400°F/200°C/gas mark 6.

2   First make the base. Melt the coconut, sugar and syrup or honey with the milk in the oven in a covered ovenproof bowl.

3   Stir in the oats, spice and orange rind and press into a well-greased 8 in. (20 cm) deep-sided cake tin – preferably loose-bottomed or with a rotating blade. Bake in the oven for 10 minutes.

4   Allow the base to cool for 15 minutes and lower the oven temperature to 325°F/170°C/gas mark 3.

5   Meanwhile make the filling. Whisk the egg whites until stiff but not dry. Stir the sugar into the orange juice.

6   Blend together the fromage frais, yogurt and egg yolks and stir in the sweetened orange juice and the rind.

7   Fold in the egg whites and pour over the base.

8   Bake in the oven at the lower temperature for about 55 minutes, until the filling is set.

9   When cool, decorate if you wish with a peak of fromage frais and a piece of fruit per serving. Refrigerate the cheesecake until you are ready to eat.

## Simple Ice Cream with Exotic Fruit Purée

*For the ice cream:*
SERVES 10–12
1 × 14 oz (400 g) tin evaporated milk
1 × 10 fl oz (300 ml) carton vegetable oil whipping cream
$\frac{1}{2}$ teaspoon vanilla essence
$\frac{1}{2}$ teaspoon mixed spice
1 oz (25 g) soft brown sugar *or* powdered artificial sweetener

*For the fruit purée:*
SERVES 4–6
1 large ripe mango *or* 3–4 ripe passion fruit
Lemon or lime juice

1   Chill the tin of milk for a few hours in the fridge.

2   Whip the milk and cream together until the mixture reaches maximum thickness.

3   Add the vanilla, spice and the sugar or artificial sweetener to taste and mix evenly.

4   Pour into a well washed-out $3\frac{1}{2}$ pint (2 litre) ice cream carton and freeze for at least 6 hours in a deep freeze.

5   Prepare the mango, if using, by cutting into quarters and

prizing the flesh from the stone. Scoop the flesh from the skin and mash or liquidize to a purée with a little lemon or lime juice. If using passion fruit – the flesh of which should be yellow and juicy with edible seeds – cut in half, scoop out the flesh and mash.

The above recipe provides more servings of ice cream than of fruit purée: eat the remaining ice cream at other meals.

Many other fruits make a delicious purée to accompany the ice cream – for example, apricots, peaches or cooked currants – red, white and black.

The ice cream can be made in a variety of flavours. Try mocca – warm a little of the evaporated milk in order to dissolve some powdered drinking chocolate and instant coffee; or rum flavouring and mixed dried fruit – the ice cream should be stirred with a folding movement when nearly set to prevent the fruit settling at the bottom.

## *Banana Fig Cake*

MAKES ABOUT 8 SLICES
3 oz (75 g) dried banana, chopped
5 oz (150 g) dried figs, chopped
5 fl oz (150 ml) apple juice
$2\frac{1}{2}$ oz (65 g) brown sugar
$3\frac{1}{2}$ fl oz (90 ml) oil
2 eggs, beaten
5 oz (150 g) fine self-raising wholemeal flour
$1\frac{1}{2}$ teaspoons mixed spice
4 fl oz (125 ml) natural yogurt

1   Simmer the banana and figs in the apple juice in a covered pan for 10 minutes.
2   Add the sugar and stir until dissolved. Leave to cool for about 45 minutes. Heat the oven to 350°F/180°C/gas mark 4.
3   Mix all the remaining ingredients with the fruit mixture and pour into a well-greased 8 in. (20 cm) cake tin
4   Bake in the oven for about 45 minutes, until firm. Cool for about 3 minutes before turning on to a wire rack.

## Mulled Wine

MAKES 8 GLASSES

$1\frac{1}{2}$ oranges
3 tablespoons brandy *or* rum
1 rounded tablespoon soft brown sugar
$2\frac{1}{2}$ wine glasses orange juice
4 cloves
1 × 75 cl bottle red table wine
1 teaspoon mixed spice

1   Cut 3 slices from the orange and cut these into quarters. Mix together the brandy, sugar and orange juice and soak the orange pieces in the mixture for about 2 hours.

2   Cut the remaining chunk of orange in two. Spike the skin of each piece with two cloves.

3   Heat the brandy mixture, red wine, spice and orange pieces stuck with cloves on the hob in a large lidded saucepan or in a microwave or slow-cooker. Bring the mixture to just below the boil – but do not boil.

4   The drink can be kept warm on a hot-plate (the one on a filter coffee maker can be used) or it can be rewarmed in a microwave as required.

The quantities can simply be halved to make 4 glasses.

# USEFUL ADDRESSES

British Diabetic Association
10 Queen Anne Street
London W1M 0BD
Tel: 01–323 1531

Coronary Prevention Group
60 Great Ormond Street
London WC1N 3HR
Tel: 01-833 3687

Vegetarian Society
53 Marlowes Road
Kensington
London W8
Tel: 01–937 7739

The leaflet *Food Additives: The Numbers Identified* and the booklet
*Food Additives: The Balanced Approach* are obtainable from:

*In England and Wales*
Ministry of Agriculture, Fisheries and Food
Publications Unit
Lion House
Willowburn Trading Estate
Alnwick
Northumberland NE66 2PF

*In Scotland*
Scottish Home and Health Department
Foods Branch
Room 44
St Andrew's House
Edinburgh EH1 3DE

A booklet, *Healthy Eating in Later Life*, is obtainable on receipt of a 9 × 6 in. (22 × 15 cm) stamped self-addressed envelope, from:

Dulcolax Healthy Eating Offer
Bury House
126–128 Cromwell Road
London SW7 4ET

A booklet entitled *Demi Veg*, on a new style of eating that is not quite vegetarian, is obtainable, on receipt of a 9 × 6 in. (22 × 15 cm) stamped self-addressed envelope, from:

The Fresh Fruit and Vegetable Information Bureau
Bury House
126–128 Cromwell Road
London SW7 4ET

# saga

# MONEY GUIDE

For all of us, retirement brings a change in our financial position. This clear, practical guide will help you plan and manage your money in the best possible way for a secure and happy retirement. It includes advice on:

- Company and private pensions
- Income and inheritance tax
- Investing in the Stock Market ● Gifts
- Insurance ● Making a will

Complete with useful addresses and information on how to get specialist advice, this easy-to-follow book will allow you to get the best possible financial deal for your long term future.

**Paul Lewis** is a freelance writer who contributes regularly to *Saga Magazine*, and is an expert on financial and legal matters.

*Other books in this series*

**Saga Property Guide**
**Saga Health Guide**
**Saga Leisure Guide**
**Saga Rights Guide**

# *saga*
## PROPERTY GUIDE

Retirement is a time when many of us reassess our housing requirements, and start to look to the future. This book gives practical common sense advice on all the concerns that most often arise, including:

- The pros and cons of moving to a smaller home
- Holiday resorts ● Sheltered Housing
- Living abroad ● Nursing homes
- Buying and selling property
- Legal and financial aspects

Concluding with lists of addresses of builders, trade and aid organizations specializing in retirement housing, this invaluable guide will equip you to take the housing decisions best suited to your needs.

**Michael Dineen** is a regular Saga contributor and writes a weekly property column for *The Observer*.

*Other books in this series*

**Saga Rights Guide**
**Saga Money Guide**
**Saga Leisure Guide**
**Saga Health Guide**

# *saga*
## RIGHTS GUIDE

This guide clearly outlines the many rights, concessions and services which become available to you on your retirement.

- Pensions, both within the UK and abroad
- Illness and disability provisions
- Help with a low income • Rate and rent rebates
- Legal aid • Motor insurance

These are just some of the issues clarified in this book. Concluding with useful addresses, and information about complaints procedures and ombudsmen, this is an essential reference book to steer you through today's complex bureaucracy.

**Paul Lewis** is a freelance writer who contributes regularly to *Saga Magazine,* and is an expert on financial and legal matters.

*Other books in this series*

**Saga Property Guide**
**Saga Health Guide**
**Saga Money Guide**
**Saga Leisure Guide**

# saga
## LEISURE GUIDE

Your retirement is the opportunity to do all those things you've hoped to do but never had the time.

- Long distance luxury cruises
- Weekend breaks ● Caravanning
- University courses ● Charity work
- New sports and pastimes

These are just some of the many ideas explored in this book. The *Saga Leisure Guide* includes a questionnaire on your qualities as a retiree and offers advice on courses to prepare you for this new phase. This is the book to ensure that your retirement is the time of your life.

**Roy Johnstone** is a freelance journalist and a regular contributor to *Saga Magazine* on leisure issues.

*Other books in this series*

**Saga Property Guide**
**Saga Health Guide**
**Saga Money Guide**
**Saga Rights Guide**